The Complete Golfer

Physical Skill and Mental Toughness

Thomas N. Dorsel, Ph.D.
Professor of Psychology
Francis Marion University

Allyn and Bacon
Boston • London • Toronto • Sydney • Tokyo • Singapore

Senior Series Editor: Suzy Spivey
Editorial Assistant: Lisa Davidson
Editorial-Production Service: Matrix Productions
Cover Designer: Suzanne Harbison
Composition Buyer: Linda Cox
Manufacturing Buyer: Aloka Rathnam

Copyright © 1996 by Allyn & Bacon
A Simon & Schuster Company
Needham Heights, Mass. 02194

Printed in the United States of America

10 9 8 7 6 5 4 3 2 1   00 99 98 97 96

Photo Credits   Figure 1–1: NASA; Figures 3–1, 3–2, 3–3, 3–5, 5–13, and 7–3: Author; the rest of the photos were taken by Kenny Smith.

To Serious Golfers—Past, Present, and Future

Contents

Foreword

If the title *The Complete Golfer: Physical Skill and Mental Toughness* caught your eye, then you are already on the road to becoming a proficient golfer. You realize that there is a physical side and a psychological side to golf and that both must be learned in order to be a complete golfer.

Books devoted to the proper mechanics of the golf swing abound. There are also a few books that focus solely on the mental side of the game. The book you are about to read presents a balanced picture of both the swing mechanics and the mental challenges of the game.

The physical and the psychological begin to interact as soon as you pick up a club. Physically, you are practicing how to stand, hold, and swing the club with your very first swipes at the ball. Psychologically, you are dealing with excitement, frustration, and pressure from your initial moments on the links. While the physical and psychological challenges of the game will evolve over time, the balance will remain the same: proper physical technique must be combined with clear thinking and control of your emotions if you are to be the complete golfer.

The importance of proper mechanics is fairly easily envisioned. But how psychology can enhance your game may need some explanation. Let me be very specific and tell you some of the ways in which psychology has helped me over the years.

I've always been dedicated to practice. However, my practice used to be purely physical. You know, pounding balls hour after hour on the range. Psychology has taught me to practice smart: how to practice efficiently and effectively, making *more* progress in *less* time.

Controlling my temper on the golf course used to be quite a challenge. If you have dabbled at all with golf, you can probably identify with my earlier frustrations. Now, thanks to psychology, I know how to control my emotions, and even how to use them to my advantage.

The application of psychology has made a considerable contribution to my success in competition. Instead of becoming overanxious and entertaining negative thoughts before a match, I now expect success and view upcoming events as another opportunity to compete and win. I understand strategy; for example, how to play patiently on the front nine while courageously attacking the back. Recovering from adversity, holding a lead, and closing out opponents are now lesser problems. I can take bad situations and turn them to my advantage in ways I never previously considered.

Confidence, relaxation, and concentration, states which are achieved by only the best in any sport, are much more within my reach these days. Psychology has also made golf more enjoyable and given me a greater appreciation for the game's beauty and challenge while demonstrating my potential for growth, not only as a golfer, but also as a person.

You may never learn all there is to know about the game of golf, but reading *The Complete Golfer: Physical Skill and Mental Toughness* will get you started in the right direction. If you then devote adequate practice to both the physical and the psychological sides of the game, you should approach your full potential as a golfer and have a game you can enjoy for a lifetime.

Golf has been a major focus in my life since I was about ten years old. Nothing consumed, absorbed, excited, and captivated me as much as golf. To this day my love for golf reminds me of General George Patton who felt compelled to ask forgiveness for his love of warfare. Perhaps my attachment to hitting a ball around a meadow is equally in need of forgiveness; but, by George, I do love it.

Acknowledgements

Appreciation is extended to Francis Marion University and Florence (SC) Country Club, along with the latter's professional golf staff and course superintendents, for their generous provision of time and materials involved in the writing of this book. Acknowledgement is also due *GOLF Magazine, GOLFWEEK, Golf Digest, and Golf Illustrated* for allowing me to use the material from my previously published works, which initially appeared in these respected publications.

I would also like to specifically thank my editors at Allyn & Bacon, especially Suzy Spivey, and at Matrix Productions, especially Colleen O'Brien and Sonya Manes; and also Francis Marion University staff members Kenny Smith for his skilled photography; Ross Fleming, Brad Wofford, and Don Chambers for their assistance with audiovisual needs; Dr. George E. Harding for his helpful suggestions and critical reading of the manuscript; and Dr. Emilie W. Cellucci for her suggestion regarding the title.

Special recognition is due Dr. Fiona J. Connor–Kuntz of Indiana University for his detailed review of the manuscript and expert recommendations. Other reviewers deserving recognition include Dr. Michael R. Griffin of Valdosta State University, Dr. E. Murray Rudisill of Old Dominion University, Dr. Ronald A. Sendre of Central Michigan University, Dr. Robert R. Pickert of the University of Minnesota, Dr. Paula Williams of the University of Southwest Louisiana, Dr. Owen Wilkinson of Ohio University, and Dr. David C. Moore of Valdosta State University.

Others who contributed to the development of the text with their innovative ideas and provision of resource material include Dr. Earl J. Kronenberger of Xavier University and F. David Whitehead of Hartsville, SC.

Most importantly, I would like to thank my wife, Sue, for her patience, support, and encouragement with this project, not to mention her insightful suggestions over the years; our children, Julie, Danny, Gina, and Chris, for their supportive interest in my work; and my father and mother, Norbert and Jean, for giving me the opportunity to practice and learn my lifelong passions: golf and psychology.

T. N. D.

Golf: A Sport Extraordinaire

Golf is an intriguing mixture of the physical, the psychological, and the philosophical. *Physically*, it requires stamina to walk four miles, and strength to swing a golf club with enough force that the ball travels a reasonable distance. At the same time, golf demands physical delicateness, allowing one to execute precise little shots requiring accuracy and finesse. Rhythmic timing is also required, which is actually more important than brute strength in getting the optimal performance out of your golf swing. Timing explains why smaller, less muscular individuals can sometimes perform better than their stronger and seemingly more powerful counterparts.

Psychologically, there are endless challenges. To begin with, golf is a complex behavior governed by the laws of learning that psychologists have studied for over a century. One's personality, decision-making ability, stress tolerance, and level of self-confidence are other psychological factors that enter into the game. Ultimately, the pure enjoyment of golf is more of a psychological phenomenon than a physical one.

But the game of golf goes even deeper than these physical and psychological considerations. Golf at its finest is a *philosophical* exercise. If the derivation of the word "philosophy" is traced to its Greek origins, it means love (*philos*) of wisdom (*sophia*). Courses in philosophy attempt to instill in the student a love of wisdom, particularly as it applies to understanding life. Golf also teaches a lot about wisdom and life. It requires patience and self-control and involves challenges and risks. Golf encourages an appreciation of beauty as well as an acceptance of strengths and shortcomings in both oneself and others. Life-long golfers are likely to emerge much the wiser for having immersed themselves in the sport.

Golf is a special game in many other ways. For example, it is the only game ever played on the moon (Figure 1-1). Stories also tell of individuals near death who were motivated to recover from their maladies because of an undying desire to return to playing golf. Legendary pro golfer Ben Hogan is a case in point. Facing death and subsequent near paralysis after a head-on collision with a bus, Hogan recuperated and went on to win many golf tournaments, including the U.S. Open Championship, in the 1950s.

FIGURE 1-1   Astronaut Alan Shepard executing a 6-iron shot on the surface of the moon.

Golf is a great equalizer. Mr. Businessman, who sits behind a desk all week, can often go out and beat the socks off a professional athlete in a member–guest tournament. Women can play right alongside men; children can challenge adults; the weak can frustrate the strong; and the elderly can continue to play competitively well into their ninth decade. How many games in all of sport can a person still enjoy and play productively at such a ripe old age?

And consider the variety in golf. In contrast to the standard, nearly identical playing fields of almost every other sport, no two golf courses in the world are alike. In fact, the same course can display very different characteristics on a daily basis because of weather conditions, the manicuring of the turf, and the way the course has been set up for play. When the dimension of how well (or how poorly) the golfer is hitting the ball on any given day is added, the variety in golf may be extended to locations on the course that the player never previously knew existed.

One final highlight of this special game is the enormous beauty of golf courses. Some of the most beautiful real estate in the world has been made even more attractive by overlaying it with the exquisiteness of a finely manicured golf course. Be it by the ocean, in the mountains, among sparkling lakes and streams, or over rolling plains and farmlands, the beauty of golf is truly breathtaking. And the challenge of these varied terrains is never ending.

MENTAL SPOTLIGHT   A Golf Course Architect's View of the Mental Side of the Game

Perhaps more than any other game, golf requires mental preparedness. Whether players have a perfect textbook swing or not, their success in competition depends on their ability to think clearly before making each shot.

To be sure, the lone golfer matches wits against the architect, the golf course, and the elements. There are no backups here, no substitutes, just a one-on-one with the course.

Three of the greatest to ever play the game had mental toughness as their trademark. People may squabble about who is really the best there ever was, but Bobby Jones, Ben Hogan, and Jack Nicklaus were thinkers extraordinaire, and all produced great victories overseas in spite of adverse conditions.

Like many of the foreign players these days who have risen to prominence, these legendary performers were able to mount a mental outlook on the game that provided them with confidence regarding their physical ability to play every shot. This permitted a mental restraining order sufficient to control their emotions and anxieties. Golf course architects should prey on those potential moments of anxiety and pressure; the great golf professional's response is to beat them at that game.

Excerpt from *Bury Me in a Pot Bunker* (pg. 218), © 1995 by Mark Shaw and Pete Dye. Reprinted by permission of Addison-Wesley Publishing Company, Inc.

Golf is truly a game for life; and like life, it isn't easy. But if you persevere, keep the game in perspective, and develop an appreciation for the many facets of the sport, it is a good bet that golf will become an important part of your life, too.

C h a p t e r **2**

The Game and the Course

Although many people already have some knowledge of the game of golf, it is essential that players be fully informed about the basic rules of the game and the field of play.

The Game

In its elementary form, golf is very simple. The game is played over a course that contains 18 holes, each of which is actually more than just a hole. A golf hole is composed of a *tee box*, which is the starting point for any given hole; a *fairway*, which is a wide pathway proceeding away from the tee; and a *green*, which is a fairly large, smooth surface at the end of the fairway where the hole is ultimately found.

The game proceeds by setting the ball on a little wooden peg called a "tee," which the golfer sticks in the ground in the tee box (Figure 2-1). From its resting point on the tee, the golfer hits the ball repeatedly along the fairway, using various golf clubs, while otherwise not touching the ball until it rolls in the hole on the green. This sequence of events is done repeatedly over 18 holes, and ultimately all the strokes are combined to generate an 18-hole score.

Par is the expected score for an expert golfer on any given hole. Golf holes are of different lengths, which determine different pars for each hole. Holes ranging up to 250 yards in length are generally assigned a par of three strokes, assuming it should take the golfer one shot to get from tee to green and two putts to get the ball in the hole. Holes ranging from 250–450 yards in length are usually considered to be par fours, allowing two shots from tee to green and two putts to finish the hole. Holes over 450 yards are generally par fives, requiring three shots to the green and again two putts.

The typical golf course ranges in total length from 5,000 to 7,000 yards and is composed of ten par fours, four par fives, and four par threes. The total par for such a course adds up to a score of 72. Par is an ideal score which very few golfers actually achieve on a regular basis. Eighteen-hole scores for beginners will be well over 100, the national average of all golfers being about 92. A score in the 80s is a very re-

FIGURE 2-1   Golfer placing "tee" in tee box. Notice how golfer uses ball rather than only his fingers to press tee into ground.

spectable accomplishment, and regular scores in the 70s are only for a select few. Expectations about score should be kept realistic, allowing golf to be fun at all levels of play.

Par is but one of the terms commonly heard around the golf course. Others referring to scores on holes include *bogey* (one stroke over par), *double bogey* and *triple bogey* (two and three strokes over par, respectively), *birdie* (one under par), and *eagle* (two under par). A *double eagle* is three under par on a hole, which usually requires hitting a long second shot into the hole on a par five. This event is so rare that it is not even listed as a regular statistical category on the Professional Golf Association (PGA) Tour, where only four double eagles were recorded in all of 1993.

The Course

As mentioned above, the golf course is basically composed of tee boxes, fairways, and greens. These features, however, will benefit from a little further elaboration.

Tee Boxes

The tee box is a closely cut grassy area, which is basically flat and the only place where the golfer is given the advantage of setting the ball on a wooden tee. The flat, well-manicured surface and the use of a tee allow for the easiest shot possible in getting off to a good start on any given hole.

There may actually be several tee boxes on each hole, each tee box positioned at different distances from the green (Figure 2-2). This arrangement allows for players of different proficiency levels to be appropriately challenged. Typically, the different tees are referred to as the *championship*, *men's*, *seniors'*, and *ladies'*, tees, although such evaluative, even prejudicial, terminology has been questioned in recent times. Consider, for example, that there are women who can hit the ball as far as men, and seniors who are still of championship caliber.

Nevertheless, whatever the tee box options are called, they serve a good purpose and should be used appropriately by golfers of different skill levels. For example, beginners should use the shorter tee boxes and only gradually move back as they improve. Similarly, older golfers should not let pride stand in the way of returning to the shorter tee boxes as the length of their shots starts to wane a bit. Using the appropriate tee boxes allows golfers of all skill levels to achieve their greatest enjoyment from the game.

Fairways

The fairway is another closely cut grassy area which is typically 20 to 60 yards wide and extends in length from 75 to 600 yards, depending on the demands of the particular golf hole. Although not cut quite as closely as the tee box, the fairway is still cut close enough

FIGURE 2-2   Three separate tee boxes for the same golf hole.

to provide for a *good lie*, which means that the ball is sitting up nicely on top of the grass. Good lies allow for easier shots, making the fairway the preferred target from the tee box. The alternative destination for the ball is *the rough*, the longer grass that borders the fairway and that may contain trees, bushes, bare spots, and any number of otherwise ungroomed areas or obstacles (Figure 2-3).

Other features, which the golfer may have to negotiate in the fairway or the rough, include lakes, streams, bunkers (depressions in the ground filled with sand and often referred to as sand traps), mounds, and variations in terrain that can sometimes produce fairly severe uphill, downhill, or sidehill lies.

Greens

Greens are the most closely cut, smoothest areas on the golf course. They vary in shape, can be flat or gently rolling, and tend to cover as much as a quarter of an acre of exquisitely cultivated land.

Greens are composed of special grasses, the finest of which is bent grass, which grows especially well in cooler climates. Bermuda grass is more common in hotter climates. Greens are often surrounded by rough, sand bunkers, mounds, and/or an occasional pond.

The special nature of greens requires considerable caution in maintaining and using them. They have to be watered and manicured constantly or they will quickly become unplayable. When a shot from the fairway hits the green, the ball may make a mark, which

FIGURE 2-3   The longer grass of the *rough* (left) compared to the shorter grass of the *fairway* (right).

has to be repaired immediately (Figure 2-4) or an unsightly scar will form on the green and the smoothness of the surface will suffer. Golfers also have to be careful to lift their spikes as they walk across a green lest they unintentionally drag them, tear the surface, and leave spike marks. It is also important to be careful around the hole, never stepping closer than within 12–18 inches of the hole when retrieving the ball. Otherwise, the edges of the hole may cave in.

One never does anything but roll the ball with a putter across the surface of a green. Other clubs, which necessarily dig into fairways, rough, and sand, are never supposed to dig into the refined surface of a green.

Regarding the golf course, in general, nothing is more aggravating than having an unnecessarily difficult shot because a previous player failed to take proper precautions in maintaining the golf course. This includes (1) patching up the little areas that shots dig up on the tee boxes or in the fairway (called "divots") by either replacing the original turf or filling the divot hole with sand; (2) smoothing out sand in bunkers with a rake; (3) repairing ball marks and spike marks on the greens, and so on.

FIGURE 2-4 Ball mark on green made by forceful landing of ball. The ball mark, or depression in the green, is fixed by using a repair tool like the one shown above. The tool is inserted repeatedly around the depression, each time lifting the top part of the tool toward the center of the depression, pulling the surrounding grass together so as to eliminate the ball mark.

Such maintenance may sound a bit tedious at first, but it becomes quite automatic after a while. More importantly, carefulness and courtesy will be greatly appreciated by fellow golfers and add to everyone's enjoyment of the game.

MENTAL SPOTLIGHT   Major Courses Tough Enough without 'Tricksters' Running Wild

At this year's Masters, as you probably recall, Fuzzy Zoeller and a number of other golfers had some rather unflattering things to say about the playing conditions for golf's major tournaments.

Zoeller suggested that tournament officials were "tricking up" the major tournament layouts, thereby taking all the fun out of the game. Sandy Lyle seemed to concur when he said that there was a fine line between a very, very tough course and being ridiculous.

It seems this issue could be viewed from various angles. For example, should golf involve trickery or unfair conditions? Probably not. Golf, like other age-old games, is a test of straightforward skill. It's not a game of guessing and surmounting tricks. Imagine a tennis match where periodically the players were surprised by the net being raised six inches at the whims of the officials.

But let's suppose that trickery were condoned. Would it take the fun out of the game? How much fun would the Super Bowl be if occasionally the ball blew up in mid-air just when the quarterback was about to strike for a touchdown? Or it might be argued that the college teams are playing much too well in the NCAA final four, so let's trick things up by loosening some of the slats in the floor so that the players might misdribble and sometimes trip and fall flat on their faces. Or protecting against another Nadia in Olympic gymnastics, let's grease the parallel bars so that nobody will ever come close to scoring another 10. Would such trickery really make watching these events more fun?

Not for me! I marvel at these outstanding performances.

Zoeller surprised officials by complaining about the conditions after shooting a spectacular 66. I can imagine what would have been said if Fuzzy had stated his opinion after shooting 80. He would have been accused of sour grapes!

Criticism must always be taken more seriously when coming from a winner than when coming from a loser. One has to think a lot more intently about beauty being skin deep if that suggestion comes from Miss America rather than from Miss Piggy!

From a psychological standpoint, however, I had to wonder what impact such comments by a player in the middle of a tournament might have on his play during the rounds yet to come. To some extent it might depend on how much the public and fellow players agreed with him. But the greater risk seemed to be that in order for Fuzzy to be right, the conditions would eventually have to treat him unfairly. Additionally, he couldn't be happy with his play from that point forward, lest he risk being accused of enjoying the very conditions which he previously criticized. Judging from Zoeller's subdued demeanor over the final two rounds and his finish well back in the pack, it would seem that either or both of these anticipated consequences may have materialized.

Is it really such a disgrace to golf and to great courses that our pros are able to achieve phenomenal performances from time to time? I don't think so. Indeed, that's what we tune in for and hope to see. Anyone who has seen the championship courses knows that they are tough enough, and can be made even tougher without appealing to trickery and unfairness.

But if we still want to make golf tougher, let's do it not by adding trickery, but by removing trickery even further from yet another aspect of the game—the equipment. Let's do away with "tricked-up" balls with special covers, centers, and dimple patterns, and super clubs with exotic grooves, flanges, and weight distribution. Why not require that everyone play with the same standard set of equipment?

Wouldn't it be nice if golf could get back to just being golf—a beautifully difficult, straightforward test of human skill!

C h a p t e r 3

Essentials on Equipment

The first step in playing golf is to obtain suitable equipment. Colleges that offer physical education classes in golf will provide for minimal equipment needs. If private lessons from a pro at a local club are involved, the pro may temporarily make some clubs available for the beginner to try out the game. If the golfer is supplying his or her own clubs, a less expensive, used set may suffice until a level of commitment to the game is reached that justifies an investment in new, personalized equipment.

New clubs should be tailored to the golfer's skill level and type of swing. To make the wisest purchases, seek the advice of a Class-A member of the Professional Golfers' Association (PGA). He or she will likely be the head golf pro at a nearby course and, ideally, should be someone who has given you lessons and, therefore, knows your game. To help in approaching this person knowledgeably, here are a few tips to keep in mind:

Clubs

The number of clubs that are allowed to be carried during a round of golf is fourteen. All fourteen do not have to be carried, and many beginners need carry only about half that many.

Clubs vary primarily in the types of clubheads they have. The clubhead is the larger end of the club which makes direct contact with the ball. There are four different types of clubs, or, more accurately, clubheads:

Woods

Traditionally, woods have been large-headed wooden clubs used for driving the ball off the tee as well as for long shots from the fairway. Ironically, many of the modern "woods" are now made of metal, but they still tend to be referred to as woods.

The woods typically range in number from one to five. They vary in clubhead size and in loft, which refers to the angle of the clubface (the part of the club which makes contact with the ball) in relation to the ground. The more closely the clubface angle approximates a right angle (perpendicular to the ground), less loft is present and the lower the clubhead will propel the ball into the air. The 1 wood, or driver, has the least degree of loft. It is intended to hit the ball low and far, with added roll along the ground from its low flight pattern. Drivers vary in loft in the range of about a seven- to 12-degree departure from a perpendicular clubface. A beginner will probably want to start with an 11- or 12-degree driver, as the additional loft should make it a little easier to get the ball airborne (Figure 3-1).

As the woods proceed from the driver through to the 5 wood, the loft increases slightly with each higher-numbered club up to about 20 degrees, thereby producing a higher flight of the ball and less distance with each increase in loft. Woods can be obtained with even greater loft, numbering as high as nine or more. The higher-numbered woods are preferred by players who feel especially comfortable playing with the woods. But most golfers don't even carry all five of the lower-numbered woods in order to stay within the 14-club limit.

Irons

The traditional iron clubs are numbered one through nine and are made of metal in the shape of a blade. Like the woods, the move from lower- to higher-numbered irons brings a gradual increase in loft starting at about 20 degrees and ranging up to about 44 de-

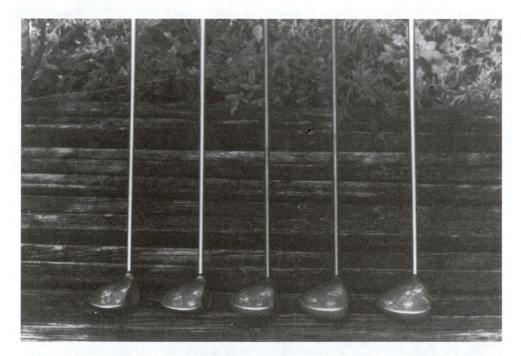

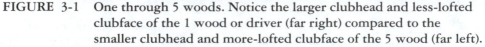

FIGURE 3-1   One through 5 woods. Notice the larger clubhead and less-lofted
clubface of the 1 wood or driver (far right) compared to the
smaller clubhead and more-lofted clubface of the 5 wood (far left).

grees. The 1 and 2 irons, like the driver, hit the ball quite low and afford some roll when the ball hits the ground. At the other extreme, the 8 and 9 irons hit the ball very high, which results in a precipitous drop and very little roll after contact with the ground (Figure 3-2).

Again, one can't carry all the irons and stay within the 14-club limit. Most golfers do not carry a 1 iron, and some prefer a 5 wood to a 2 iron, as their functions overlap to some extent. This is something golfers get a feel for and decide for themselves once they have played the game for a while.

Wedges

The wedge is an iron club with varying degrees of loft ranging from 48 to 64 degrees (Figure 3-3). All of these clubs are intended to hit the ball very high, stopping it quickly on the green. The 48-degree pitching wedge is designed for shots from the fairway and rough within about 100 yards distance from the green. The 56-degree sand wedge is specially designed to slide under the ball in the sand, thereby floating the ball airborne on a gentle wave of sand (Figure 3-4). The sand wedge can also be useful from fairway and rough close to the green, particularly when the shot requires getting up and over an obstacle and stopping the ball quickly on the green.

FIGURE 3-2   One through 9 irons. Notice the increasing lofts of the clubfaces
progressing from the 1 iron (far right) through the 9 iron (far left).

FIGURE 3-3   Four wedges with lofts (from right to left) of 48, 56, 60, and 64 degrees.

FIGURE 3-4   Player blasting out of sand.

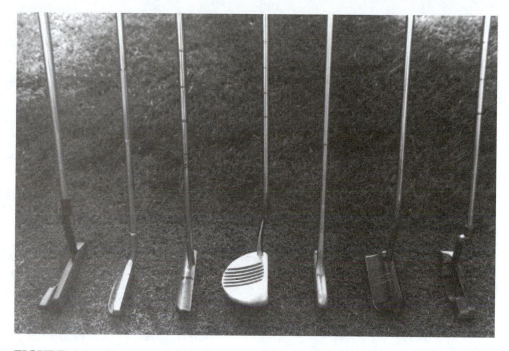

FIGURE 3-5   Several examples of the wide variety of putter styles.

More recent wedges appearing on the golf scene are the 60- to 64-degree lob wedges, which are used like the sand wedge around the green but hit the ball even higher and stop it even more quickly than the traditional sand wedge.

Wedge play has become increasingly important in the expert golfer's arsenal of shots. Therefore, golfers may carry as many as three or four wedges to handle all the varied demands of the short game around the green. Of course, for every wedge that is added, another club must be given up in order to stay within the 14-club limit.

Putter

The putter is actually the least lofted club in the bag, ranging from virtually no loft (perpendicular to the ground) to about five degrees of loft. In effect, the face of the putter is square to the ground, so that it can be used to roll the ball smoothly across the putting surface. Putters come in all shapes and sizes (Figure 3-5), and the one which is selected is very much a matter of personal preference. Try a number of putters until one is found that looks and feels good and, most importantly, gets the ball reliably in the hole.

Shafts and Grips

In distinguishing among clubs, the focus to this point has been on the descriptive features and functions of the heads of the clubs. There are, however, two other important features of clubs: shafts and grips.

Shafts

The shaft is the thin, cylindrical rod that leads from the golfer's hands to the clubhead. Early in the development of clubs, shafts were made of hickory wood. Later they were made of steel, and gradually the steel was made lighter and lighter. Now, clubmakers have developed shafts of still lighter materials, such as graphite and titanium. The idea is to take as much of the overall weight of the club out of the shaft and put it down into the head of the club, the part which actually strikes the ball.

Modern, lightweight shafts, along with innovative clubhead designs that often accompany them, can be effective and help the golfer considerably. This new equipment can also be expensive and therefore requires a lot of shopping around to find the right club at the right price.

As a beginner, there is no need to worry about exotic equipment. Until one is making good contact with the ball on a consistent basis, the more advanced clubs won't help anyway. And, for that matter, the ball will travel quite nicely if good contact is made with any club—old-fashioned or modern, traditional or high tech. The newer clubs are just a little easier to hit reliably, and most golfers eventually want them so as to get every advantage they can. Still, it is frugal to wait until one's game has improved to the point where the full benefits of the more expensive equipment can be appreciated.

One last thing to mention before leaving this section on shafts is the lie of the club—that is, the angle at which the shaft enters the clubhead. The shaft-clubhead angle, in conjunction with the height of the player and the way the player stands up to the ball, determines how squarely the clubhead rests on the ground. It is important for the clubhead to rest squarely on the ground so that the player has as much clubface as possible for making contact with the ball.

Some club manufacturers now give golfers a choice among upright (steep angle), regular (moderate angle), and flat (shallow angle) lies in ordering clubs. This consideration may be important for even beginning golfers who are either very short or very tall.

Grips

The grip is a piece of soft material that the golfer holds at the opposite end of the shaft from the clubhead. Early grips were made of leather but gradually shifted to rubber, which was easier to install and easier to keep in good playing condition. A further advance beyond the simple rubber grip was the cord grip, which included thin strips of cord embedded in the rubber in an effort to prevent any slippage in the hands.

Cord grips as well as some of the simple rubber grips, however, did not feel quite as soft as leather. They could be harsh on the hands, creating blisters unless a golf glove was worn (see following). Fortunately, the best of both worlds has recently been achieved with the advent of synthetic grips that feel as soft as leather.

The grip is of utmost importance, because a firm hold on the club is necessary to ensure that the club doesn't turn in the hands during the golf swing or at contact with the ball. Buying quality grips, cleaning them regularly, and replacing them when they can't be rejuvenated to a consistent, tacky feel generate confidence in holding the club.

Gloves

Whether leather, rubber, cord, or the new synthetic grips are used, wearing a golf glove may still be desirable for enhancing the hold on the club. A single golf glove is customarily worn on the golfer's leading hand, the hand closest to the target when the golfer is standing next to the ball. Both hands should be solidly on the club, but it is particularly important that there be no slippage in the leading hand, since it is the appendage which provides the golf swing with direction. In contrast, the following hand, the one farthest from the target, provides power which can suffer a little more error than can direction.

Balls

Balls come in as many varieties as clubs, but the choice of balls is less important than the choice of clubs. For beginners, ball selection is primarily a matter of durability and cost containment. Beginners run the risk of hitting balls off center and damaging them. They also frequently lose balls, which can be quite expensive. Therefore, inexpensive, durable balls are recommended for beginners. For the advanced player, however, ball selection might be a somewhat more important consideration, although probably not nearly as important as the golf ball industry would have golfers think. The main issues for advanced players involve differences in distance, spin, and feel among the various brands and models of golf balls.

Balls vary in terms of compression value and the types of cover they have, which respectively determine how far the ball will travel and how much spin is imparted for stopping the ball on the green. Compression refers to how much the ball is squashed by the impact of the clubhead. The ball has to compress to a certain degree in order to spring off the clubface. When an optimal amount of compression is achieved, maximal distance will be obtained.

The compression indexes used by the golf ball industry are 100, 90, and 80. Balls of 100-compression value are for stronger golfers who hit the ball very hard. They can get optimal compression out of this ball and therefore more distance than they might from a ball of lower compression. The average golfer is likely to get the best performance from a 90-compression ball. Weaker golfers may want to try 80-compression balls. In colder weather, all golfers can benefit from moving down one level in compression value (i.e., from 100 to 90 or from 90 to 80) because the ball does not compress as easily in lower temperatures.

As far as the cover goes, balata-covered balls are slightly softer than other balls, which may translate into softer feel when the clubface makes contact with the ball. Balata balls also generate more spin for stopping the ball more quickly on the green. Balata balls tend to travel a little less far than other balls, and they also become damaged more quickly because of the softer cover.

Surlyn-covered balls are harder and tougher, providing more distance and greater durability. But the soft feel at impact and the greater spin when the ball hits the green may be sacrificed when using the surlyn ball.

As with rubber grips with leather feel, there are now surlyn, distance-generating balls purported to have balata feel and action. Golfers should ultimately read the manufacturers' labels, try a few different varieties of balls, and see which ones feel comfortable and encourage confidence. Conveniently, golfers find a lot of lost balls, which provide ample opportunity to try a vast variety of brands and types at no cost. It may take years to settle on a preferred type of ball.

Although the choice of a particular ball may not be that critical, it is important to switch to a new ball every once in a while, whatever the brand or model might be. Any ball will lose its liveliness after many holes of play, giving a new ball a distinct advantage over an old ball. A psychological lift may also result from looking down at a bright new ball and imagining all that stored-up energy about to explode off of the clubface.

Shoes

Beginners can play in a nice pair of gym shoes with modest tread on the bottom. Some tread is helpful in keeping one's feet from twisting out of position on the ground. On the other hand, too much tread could damage the greens.

A pair of golf shoes with little spikes on the bottom is ultimately the best way to facilitate good footing during the golf swing. The type of shoes bought, in my opinion, is mainly a matter of style and preference, as most golf shoes on the market today seem to be built more for riding in golf cars than for walking. That is, few shoes, if any, on the market seem to have the supportive construction or overall quality necessary to provide comfort and durability over many rounds of walking the golf course. Basically, when you start shopping for golf shoes, expect to find stylish dress shoes (with little spikes in the bottom) on the shelves. If walking is the intended mode of transportation around the course, I suggest inserting personal orthotics in your golf shoes for support. Also, if you walk the course several times per week, expect to replace your golf shoes every year or so. On the more optimistic side, as more and more people insist on walking when they play, manufacturers will come out with golf shoes offering better support and more durable construction.

Bags

Golf bags have evolved over the years from the simplest of canvas tubes that held only a few clubs and were easily carried to the huge, exotic, leather cylindrical bins that can hold half a pro shop full of clubs and barely be carried to the motorized golf car necessary to haul them around. Of course, there are many varieties in between which may serve the dual purposes of walking and golf car play.

If walking is the dominant form of play, super light bags are available which can considerably lighten the load. There are also new conveniences for carrying bags, such as double shoulder straps to distribute the weight over both shoulders when the bag is being carried, and pop-out legs which enable the bag to stand upright when it is set on the ground. A bag should also have good balance so that the clubs are not tending to fall forward and out of the bag as it is carried. A supporting rod from the top to the bottom of the bag is also important so that the bag does not collapse when set on the ground or mounted on a golf car or pull cart (i.e., a simple little buggy with wheels and a handle used for rolling a bag of clubs around the course).

Other features that might be noted are outside pockets on the bag. Consider whether the pockets are numerous enough and big enough to accommodate balls, tees, and whatever else might need to be stored. Does a full pocket of balls impinge on space for shafts on the inside of the bag?

Another feature to consider is the dividers in the club compartment of the bag. Is the bag divided into enough sections? Are the sections big enough? It is not advisable to cram clubs into a bag, thereby scraping the grips and shafts against each other.

One last consideration is clubhead covers. Wooden-headed clubs have historically benefitted from protection provided by covers. But now graphite shafts also require protection provided by long sock-like covers, which not only protect the clubhead but also extend down the shaft about 12 inches. Iron covers are usually considered a nuisance, but the meticulous golfer may also want to consider them, especially for an expensive new set of irons that the golfer intends to keep in service for years to come.

Cost

So, how much does all this cost? A fair question, and one all golfers have to regularly contend with.

A used set of clubs might cost less than $100. This will probably be a very old set, yet not inappropriate for just trying out the game. A modern, high-quality used set is likely to cost between $300 and $500. The sky's the limit on a new set of clubs, although a very good set should be obtainable for under $1000.

Specialty clubs, especially the new exotic drivers with large heads and high-tech shafts, can be expensive, as mentioned earlier. Sometimes for the avid golfer, it is worth spending upwards of $200 to get that special driver that provides an extra 20 or 30 yards when hit well. And then there is the used market, again. Those same avid golfers can get tired of their latest toy about as quickly as it turned them on. So wait a few months and a great bargain may be found.

Good quality golf balls can be purchased in discount golf stores for around $18 per dozen. It's much more expensive if smaller numbers (called a "sleeve" of three balls) are bought at the pro shop on the way to the first tee.

The cost of golf shoes is comparable to a pair of dress shoes, which as alluded to earlier is basically what they are. Typically, $50– $100 is required for a decent pair of shoes, although a beginner pair may be found at a discount store for under $25.

Golf gloves can cost from $5– $20, and they wear out quite quickly. That's why the investment in softer grips which do not require as much use of a glove may be a wise one. Playing without a glove is not only cheaper in the long run, but more consistent feel for the club might be obtained by avoiding the gradually wearing-out texture of a glove between one's hands and the grip. One last consideration is that the more golf played, the tougher the hands get, thereby further diminishing need for a glove.

The Mental Side of Equipment

Curiously, there is a mental side to the choice of equipment. The look and feel of equipment—be it clubs, balls, or shoes—can generate confidence in the golfer. When looking down at a shiny new clubhead and a lively new ball, the golfer gets the feeling that a favorable outcome is a sure thing because of such beautiful equipment. Even a new pair of shoes can provide an appearance and feeling of solidness.

The same effect can be generated to a certain degree by keeping one's less-than-new clubs and balls clean and shiny, as well as by polishing one's shoes regularly. And don't forget to replace worn spikes on your shoes in order to maintain truly solid footing as well as that psychological feeling of stability.

The feelings generated by the appearance of equipment might be more important in encouraging an effective swing than the actual physical dynamics of the equipment itself. If a golfer feels confident and relaxed with the equipment being used, he or she will be more likely to make a good golf swing, which, of course, is the all-important factor.

Another mental factor in choosing equipment is to take a scientific approach to evaluating one's options. Too often, players will pick up a club that looks attractive, go out and hit a few shots with it on the driving range, and impulsively buy it, only to find out later that it doesn't perform any better in the long run than did their old clubs.

A better way to evaluate clubs is the following: If it's drivers you're testing for distance, do a controlled test with all other variables held constant except the type of driver. For example, take six new balls of the same kind (which controls for age and type of ball), go out to a level fairway on the course (which controls for amount of roll), and hit a couple of balls with each driver. Rotate the drivers on repeated trials, hitting different ones first, second, and third (which controls for warm-up effects in hitting repeated shots). Note the accuracy of each shot in relation to a given target, and step off the distances. Be sure that each ball is marked distinctively so as to easily identify which ball was hit with which driver. Do this for several repetitions, and an objective, scientific assessment of the accuracy and length of each driver should be achieved.

This procedure may seem a bit extravagant and tedious. But remember that an important and expensive investment is about to be made, and a few new balls as well as a little time and effort may be well worth it in terms of money saved and performance gained.

It should also be noted that although pro shop merchandise is sometimes more expensive than that obtained at a discount store, the pro shop may provide the best opportunity to try out clubs before buying. A slightly more expensive club that you know you like may prove cheaper in the long run than a discount product of which you are uncertain.

C h a p t e r 4

Basic Skills

With this overview of the game, the course, and the equipment intact, the time has come to learn the basics of the golf swing. The basics include the *grip, stance, body position,* and *swing.*

Ernest Jones (1951) says the golf swing is natural and easy. It basically comes down to simply swinging the clubhead. But before attempting to understand and implement the concept of "swinging the clubhead," the golfer must first learn how to address the ball— that is, how to hold the club, assume the proper stance next to the ball, and position the body in a way that allows for a natural swing.

As most golfers play right-handed (i.e., with their right side farthest from the target as they stand next to the ball), this book has been written from a right-handed player's perspective. Left-handed players should transpose words such as left and right at those points in the text where orientation is a factor.

Grip

The word *grip* was used in the *Equipment* chapter (Chapter Three) to denote the soft material at the end of the club shaft opposite the clubhead; that is, the material that serves as the handle for the club. The word *grip* is also used for the action of the golfer in holding onto the club. In other words, the golfer "grips" the "grip" of the club. This gripping action of the golfer is what is described next.

Harvey Penick, the popular teacher of golf stars Tom Kite and Ben Crenshaw, states in his *Little Red Book* (1992) that "if you have a bad grip, you don't want a good swing" (p. 30). In other words, the grip is so basic to the foundation of the swing that, if it is incorrect, the swing will necessarily have to be incorrect to compensate. On the other hand, if the grip is correct, a correct swing comes more easily and with less conscious effort. The grip is so important that when Pete Rose took up golf after his baseball playing days, he said his first lesson consisted of spending a couple of hours working on nothing but the grip.

21

**MENTAL SPOTLIGHT   Golf a Backward Game with
                      Many Contradictions**

Putting is only one element of golf that goes against the grain. The sport as a whole is a game of opposites, ironies, contrasts, contradictions, and unexpected surprises.

Unlike most games, where a victory stems from a high score, the victor in golf is the player with the lowest score. Not a major difficulty, but curious nonetheless.

If you had no familiarity with golf clubs, wouldn't you think that you would get more distance out of a higher numbered club? Not in golf. The higher the club's number, the less distance you get, and vice versa.

Mechanically, there is no end to the apparent contradictions that emerge from swinging the club. If you hit down on the ball, the ball is more likely to go up. In contrast, if you try to lift the ball, it will often shoot along the ground, the result of a "skulled" or "topped" shot.

Assuming you eventually get the ball airborne, an interesting set of opposing forces influence its flight. If a right-handed player swings the club on a plane toward the left of the target, the ball will likely slice to the right. In contrast, if the plane of the swing is toward the right of the target, the ball will likely hook left. What naive golfer would think this to be the case? Slicers find it so hard to believe that they continue to yank the club to the left, only to see the ball banana even farther right.

Still another surprise in the area of mechanics involves swing velocity. You don't have to swing hard to hit the ball a long way. In fact, a light swing will usually result in greater distance than a hard swing as timing and contact are at least as important as clubhead speed.

A long-driving champion was once instructed to hit a ball as hard as he could while a machine clocked his clubhead speed. All he could muster was a velocity of 101 mph. Then he was told to take his normal swing, which registered at 167 mph. Surely the smooth rhythm of his normal swing contributed to the greater clubhead speed, probably resulting in crisp contact with the ball.

Lastly, the biggest irony of them all: If you look up, you probably won't see much in terms of a productive shot. On the other hand, if you keep your head down, you're more likely to hit a shot that warrants observation.

Golf is a fascinating game of opposites, ironies, contrasts, contradictions, and sometimes, pleasant surprises. It might seem as though you're going against the grain at times, but if you have faith, the golf gods will reward you.

A fundamental of the grip is the two hands working together as a unit. To accomplish a unified grip, take a 5 iron, set the sole (bottom) of the clubhead flat on the ground about 12 inches in front of the instep of your left foot, and rest the other end of the club against your left thigh (Figure 4-1). Now, reach down with your left hand like you are going to shake hands with the club. This should result in the bottom of the grip (the club's handle) resting in the curled fingers of the left hand, the palm of the left hand being somewhat on top of the grip, and the left thumb resting slightly to the right of the top of the grip (Figure 4-2). It is very important that the club rest in the curled fingers of the hand, rather than in the palm, and that the last three fingers of the left hand maintain a firm hold on the club throughout the swing (Figure 4-3).

To encourage the hands working together, the right hand is now placed on the grip below the left hand so that the little finger on the right hand either overlaps the forefinger of the left hand or interlocks with it (Figure 4-4). The overlapping grip is widely used and attributed to British golfing legend Harry Vardon (1905). Thus it is called the Vardon grip.

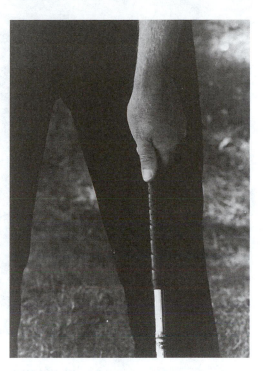

FIGURE 4-1   Sole of clubhead lying flat on ground with grip of club resting against left thigh.

FIGURE 4-2   **Golfer's left hand on grip. Notice how the thumb is turned slightly to the golfer's right of an imaginary line down the top of the club's grip and shaft. Consistent with this thumb position, only three knuckles of the left hand are visible to the golfer when looking down at the grip.**

Whether the overlapping or interlocking version of the grip is used, the bottom of the grip again rests in the curled fingers of the right hand (Figure 4-4) while (and this is very important) the right palm completely covers the left thumb. The right thumb is positioned slightly to the left of the top of the grip, resting gently against the right forefinger (Figure 4-5).

The end result of the above placement of the hands on the club is that the palms of the hands are basically facing each other (allowing for the fact that right palm is below the left palm on the grip). In addition, the back of the golfer's left hand and the palm of the right hand are facing the target.

Make sure the entire left hand is on the grip. That is, don't let the heel of the left hand be dangling off the end of the club. Grip pressure should be light, as opposed to

FIGURE 4-3   A firm hold with the last three fingers of the left hand is critical to a solid golf swing.

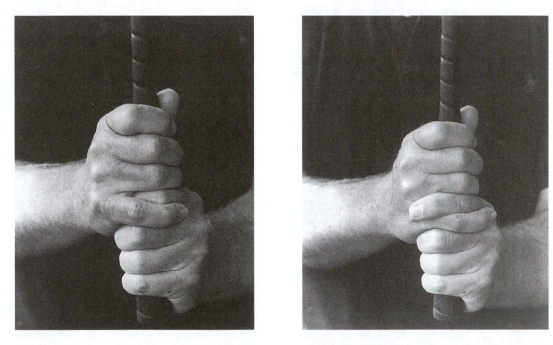

FIGURE 4-4   Comparison of *overlapping* grip (left) and *interlocking* grip (right).

FIGURE 4-5   Complete grip with the intended target to the golfer's left. Notice how the right hand is snugly against the left hand, entirely covering the left thumb. The right thumb is slightly to the golfer's left of an imaginary line down the top of the club's grip and shaft. The right thumb is also resting against the right forefinger which is curled underneath the grip of the club.

tight or loose. Sam Snead said that the club should be held like one would hold a bird—not so tight that the bird is squeezed to death, nor so loose that it can fly away. Any pressure exerted, as stated earlier, is focused on the last three fingers of the left hand, the ones at the very top of the grip. These fingers keep the club snug in the hand, particularly at the top of the swing and during the follow through. The feeling for the club transmitted through the thumb and forefinger of each hand is also important, as these fingers help you perceive the swinging motion of the clubhead during the swing, according to Ernest Jones (1951).

Stance

The stance is second only to the grip in order of fundamental importance. No matter how well the club is gripped or the ball is struck, it is not likely to go in the intended direction unless the shot is aimed correctly. The stance is the primary vehicle for aiming and, unfortunately, creates frequent errors among beginners and veterans alike.

The basic *square stance* (Figure 4-6) involves spreading the feet about the width of the shoulders with the toes of the shoes (as well as the hips and shoulders) positioned parallel to the target line. Be sure not to spread the feet too wide, as this will inhibit the body turn during the swing. On the other hand, if the feet are too close together, the stability of the stance and swing will be reduced. Although the right foot is typically placed square to the target line, it is permissible to angle the left foot as much as 30–45 degrees toward the target in order to facilitate turning the body as the club is swung through to the target. Whether the left foot is placed square to the target line or angled, it should remain stable at that angle throughout the swing and not slide around. Golf shoes are helpful in this regard.

The weight of the body should be focused on the insteps of the feet, slightly toward the balls of the feet. This will encourage lateral stability and a slight forward lean during the swing. The alternatives would be (1) to allow the weight of the body to roll over to the outsides of the feet, which would result in swaying during the swing; or (2) to have the weight out on the toes or back on the heels, which might interfere with the power, tempo, and plane of the swing.

Important variations to the square stance include the *open stance*, which involves pulling the left foot, hip, and shoulder back slightly from their positions parallel to the tar-

FIGURE 4-6   Square stance. With the slightly leaning tree trunk in the distance as the target line, note how the toes of the golfer's shoes (as well as his hips and shoulders) are on a line parallel to the target line.

FIGURE 4-7   Comparison of open stance (left) and closed stance (right). Both are similar to the square stance with the following exceptions: The open stance involves the golfer's left foot, hip, and shoulder being pulled back slightly from the intended target line; the closed stance involves the golfer's right foot, hip, and shoulder being pulled back slightly from the intended target line.

get line; and the *closed stance*, which involves pulling the right foot, hip, and shoulder back slightly from their positions parallel to the target line (Figure 4-7). The functions of the open and closed stances will be discussed in Chapter 5 under the headings of *fading* and *drawing* the ball.

Body Position

Once the club is gripped properly and the proper stance is assumed, the next move is to stand up straight and flex the knees as if to begin sitting down in a chair. The knees are the shock absorbers of the swing and cannot absorb any shock if they are locked back in their sockets. On the other hand, don't flex them too much so as to restrict the movement and arc of the swing. Just assume a slight knee flex that would be barely noticeable to an observer (Figure 4-6).

With the knees flexed and the weight of the body focused on the insteps/balls of the feet as described above, bend forward at the waist slightly (about 10 degrees) with back kept straight and chin up (Figure 4-8). This posture might be achieved by sticking the but-

FIGURE 4-8   Body position viewed from behind target line.

tocks out a bit while at the same time looking down your nose at the ball. The posture to avoid is that of hunching over the ball with a curved spine and pressing the chin against the chest as if trying to look at the ball over the top of a pair of glasses.

The end result of the above body position is that knees are flexed, spine is straight, and arms are hanging down fairly straight from the shoulders. This leaves the hands about 4–6 inches out from the inside of the left thigh. With the ball positioned somewhere between the middle of the stance and the left heel, the hands are slightly ahead of the ball and just inside the left thigh.

If someone were standing across the ball from the golfer and looking at the left arm and the shaft of the club, the arm and shaft would appear to form a straight line. That is, there would be no bend in the left elbow and no bend in the left wrist where the face of a wristwatch would normally be (Figure 4-9).

Viewed from behind the ball, looking down the target line, there is a slight wrist break downward in the line formed by the left arm and the club shaft (Figure 4-8). It is very important that the hands not be elevated as viewed from this angle. Let the hands hang down from the shoulders to create a kind of sag between the shoulders and the clubhead.

FIGURE 4-9   Body position showing straight left arm, left wrist, and clubshaft.

Swing Plane

Although the proper grip, stance, and body position of the golfer are all generally agreed upon by the master teachers of golf, there seem to be as many different views on how to maneuver the club as there are master teachers. Before describing some of these different viewpoints, however, there are a few general principles about the golf swing to keep in mind.

Head Position

A key principle of the swing is that the golfer's head stays basically in the same position, oriented toward the ball throughout the swing. This doesn't mean rigidly still, as there may be a slight turning movement of the head and maybe even a bit of lateral movement. It also does not mean keeping the head down in the sense of pressing one's chin against the chest and locking it there. Remember what was said earlier about looking down one's nose at the ball, which means the chin has to be up and away from the chest so that the club seems to pass underneath it.

One way to maintain proper head position is to keep the proverbial "eye on the ball." In most sports, successful players might be distinguished from their less successful coun-

MENTAL SPOTLIGHT   Offbeat Advice Interests Readers, but May Spur Remedial Lessons

From time to time, new ideas are advanced about golf that, at least, give the impression of violating established principles of the game.

I remember a solid teaching pro, who was in the trenches daily with his struggling and confused students, half-heartedly rejoicing: "I love it when these new ideas come out—my number of lessons triple!" In other words, people get their swings so screwed up that lessons are inevitable.

The latest offbeat suggestions in this regard were included in a recent issue of a national golf magazine. Among other things, the article suggested that it is a myth to think that one should not sway, should keep one's head down, and should keep the left arm straight.

Indeed, it may be true that an entirely adequate golf swing can involve some lateral movement, as well as a slight bend in the left arm. It may be further true that "keeping your head down" is not the best terminology for what one is to do with one's head during the swing.

But, is it wise to suggest to average golfers, or even to experts, that they abandon these useful images? What is the golfer supposed to do—make an effort to sway, bend the left arm, and lift his or her head up? This, of course, is not what the authors intended. But, then, why even allude to it?

Golfers need to try to stay perfectly still in order to stay within minimal swaying tolerances that are allowable in a solid swing. They have to feel like they are keeping their left arm straight, in order for it to bend the minimal amount that is reasonable in a golf swing. Imagine how much swaying and bending would occur if the golfer quit paying attention to these fundamentals, or, even worse, made an effort to sway and bend the left arm.

Admittedly, "keeping one's head down" is a somewhat inaccurate description of what should happen in this regard. That is, one is not supposed to press one's chin down against one's chest and keep it frozen there, thereby restricting one's shoulder movement during the swing. A more accurate description of what is supposed to occur in this regard might be to "keep your eye on the ball" throughout the swing, or at least until you are sure that the ball has left its resting place. The general notion of "keeping your head down" captures this fundamental for most golfers. If there is concern over inappropriate chin position during the swing, then that issue should be addressed directly. But don't suggest to the average golfer that it is a myth to keep one's head down during the golf swing.

In conclusion, golf authors should avoid sensationalism in presenting their ideas and, instead, get directly to the point regarding their insights into the golf swing. Readers should beware of any suggestions that run counter to established golf-swing principles that have stood the test of time. And teaching pros should increase their availability for lessons whenever it becomes evident that these two other suggestions are not being heeded.

terparts by the formers' ability to maintain an intense visual focus on the ball which they are about to either hit or catch. For example, great hitters in baseball follow the pitched ball all the way to the bat. Accomplished receivers in football visually track the ball all the way into the hands.

Such an intense focus on the ball in golf might be exemplified by a golfer's visually locking in on a particular spot on the ball (maybe the back of the ball, or a letter in the logo on the ball, or even one little dimple on the ball) and maintaining that focus until after the ball is airborne. In effect, a feeling is generated of having seen the clubhead hit the ball before viewing the result. It might help to imagine saying something after impact such as, "The ball is gone," before looking up to see the actual flight of the ball.

Weight Transfer

A second key principle is that the backswing involves a transfer of about 70 percent of the body's weight to the instep of the right foot. During this weight transfer, it is important that the right knee maintain the flexed position assumed initially at address. Otherwise, the backswing will be thrown off of its proper plane due to the right knee locking back in its socket or swaying laterally.

Subsequently, the forward swing involves virtually a 100 percent weight shift to the left side. At completion, the golfer is standing straight up on the left foot facing the target, with the right heel raised and the right toe resting on the ground for balance.

The weight shift to the right side and then back to the left is a concomitant of rhythmically swinging the clubhead. The shifting of weight contributes to the natural movement and creation of power in the golf swing.

Coiling Action

The above weight transfer occurs with a coiling action of the body, as opposed to a swaying action. Imagine one's hips turning in a barrel or the body movement of a pitcher throwing a slightly underhand, sidearm pitch (i.e., a submarine pitch). The golfer stays centered over the ball, rotating around some central reference point such as the spine or the sternum. Keeping one's head in position, as discussed earlier, contributes nicely to this coiling movement.

Relaxation

The last key component is to relax during all this action. This is not to suggest merely relaxing and having a good time. Rather, the body must be relaxed to the extent that it can flow fluidly though the coiling weight shift described above. Proper relaxation contributes to the maximum generation of power and accuracy. Said another way, the golf swing will have the most snap and pop to it (and maybe even a little crackle!), if it is relaxed through that exhilarating moment of focused energy at impact with the ball. The swing will also be more likely to stay on line toward the target.

Now for the Actual Swing!

When it comes to describing the desired path of the club around the body, a picture is indeed worth a thousand words. Therefore, the following series of photographs will provide stop-action snapshots of the various phases of the swing:

Addressing the Ball

The player begins the address from behind the ball, looking down the target line. As the player approaches the ball, the clubhead is placed immediately behind the ball, squarely on the target line. The proper grip, stance, and body position described earlier in the chapter are assumed as the player positions himself next to the ball (Figure 4-10). At this point, the right elbow is tucked in toward the body to promote a unified movement of arms and body during the swing.

MENTAL SPOTLIGHT   Relax!

Another three-putt! This lousy game. I tell you what I'm going to do: I'm going to grab my driver on the next tee and crush the longest tee shot of my life. I'll kill it. I mean I'm really going to hammer it. . . .

A little tense on the links lately? That's okay, it means you're normal. One of the things that makes golf wonderful (and awful) is that it can drive you bananas. A couple of bad shots, a series of good shots—both can wear on your nerves until you're tighter than a guitar string. And tension, both mental and physical, can damage your score by quickening your tempo, constricting your swing and throwing off your normally steady putting stroke.

When you're relaxed, however, your muscles are loose and highly effective; you have the ability to focus on each shot and, undoubtedly, you enjoy the game more.

Wouldn't it be great, then, if you could flip a "relax switch" whenever you feel tension building on (or off) the golf course? In a way, you can. Relaxation is a skill you can acquire. By devoting 30 minutes three days a week practicing the following relaxation techniques, you can train yourself to relieve tension simply by switching to the "relaxation mode."

Deep Breathing

The simplest way to begin is by breathing deeply, but there's more to it than taking a big breath and blowing it out. Try deep breathing this way:

While sitting comfortably upright in a straight-backed chair with your feet on the floor, place one hand on your abdomen. Take a slow, deep breath and feel your abdomen expand, hold it, then slowly let the air out as your abdomen falls. Do this exercise repeatedly, gathering the tension from your body each time you breathe in and letting it seep out each time you exhale.

This is the normal way you breathe when you're not paying attention to the process. When consciously taking a deep breath, you usually inhale by sucking in your stomach and expanding your chest, then do the opposite while exhaling. This conscious deep breath is unnatural and not conducive to relaxation. Practice breathing from your abdomen for the first five minutes of your relaxation session.

Progressive Muscle Relaxation

Place your hands in your lap or on the arms of the chair. Be sure not to cross your legs, clasp your hands or fold your arms in any way. Leave all body parts free to operate independently.

Focus on your right foot. Contract it for 10 seconds. Then say to yourself, "Relax," and half a second later, let the tension go quickly, as if you were dropping something. For the exercise to work, you must follow this sequence precisely.

Repeat this procedure twice with your right foot, then your left foot. Tense the left foot, hold for 10 seconds, say "Relax" and quickly let go of the tightness.

Do this twice with every part of your body, including both large and small muscle groups. The sequence might be: feet, calves, thighs, buttocks (tighten those buns so they lift you out of the chair, and then let them go and sink back), torso, neck, mouth, cheekbones and eyes (squint and close your eyes hard), forehead, biceps, forearms, hands and fingers. Remember to bypass any strained parts of your body.

This part of the workout, which should last about 20 minutes, teaches your body the feeling of relaxation. Furthermore, associating the word "Relax" with this sensation will eventually let you say the word and call up the feeling without tensing up.

Autogenic Training

To extend and enhance your relaxation, focus on your hands. Repeat to yourself, "My hands are heavy and relaxed." Once you are aware of the heaviness of your hands, repeat to yourself, "My hands are warm and comfortable." The sensation of warmth in the hands is a natural response to focusing on the extremities, so don't be surprised if you notice a warm pulsation in your fingers as you concentrate on your hands. Five minutes of autogenic training will wrap up your 30-minute session.

Taking It to the Course

Each time you perform these exercises, you should relax more quickly. Relaxation is a learned skill, like golf and other things we do. As with drives, wedges and putts, the more you practice, the better you'll get. Keep at it and after many practice sessions, simply thinking "Relax" will help you let go and make a more relaxed swing.

FIGURE 4-10   **Addressing the ball.**

Initiating the Backswing

The backswing is begun by slowly swinging the clubhead away from the target with a coiling action of the shoulders, torso, and hips, along with no lateral movement of the head, spine, or right knee (Figure 4-11). Notice that as the body coils, the toe (the front tip) of the clubhead points skyward when the club is about hip high in the backswing.

Completing the Backswing

As the clubhead is swung using the proper grip, the wrists naturally hinge or cock at the top of the backswing, the left shoulder comes under the chin, and the left arm remains fairly straight (Figure 4-12). The completed backswing finds the shaft of the club parallel to the ground and pointing toward the target. The body's weight is now concentrated on the instep/heel of the right foot, and the right knee is dynamically flexed and ready to spring forward.

Initiating the Forward Swing

The forward move is the key action in the swing, and probably the most theoretically diverse in terms of how to initiate it (Figure 4-13). The forward swing of the clubhead is most simply described as merely uncoiling what was previously coiled on the backswing. This uncoiling action, which results in nearly all of the body's weight being transferred

FIGURE 4-11   Initiating the backswing.

rapidly to the left side, might be initiated in one of several ways. Each of these ways has its proponents among the myriad modern-day teachers as well as among teachers from different eras in the history of golf. Each new golfer has to experiment and see which swing keys work for him or her:

1. Swinging the clubhead. Ernest Jones (1951) believed that if the golfer simply focused on the feeling of a heavy clubhead being swung in a relaxed fashion under the chin and toward the target, the body's weight should cooperatively shift left along with the swinging clubhead. Harvey Penick (1992) seems to agree when he suggests swinging the club with the same motion as you would a weed cutter—just back and forth with a natural, relaxed, balanced, rhythmic swinging action.

Some images that might help in generating this swinging motion of a heavy clubhead are the action of a park swing, or the rotation of a tether ball around its pole, or the weighted ball of a hammer thrower. Reflect for a moment on the force generated by these various swinging actions. It would not be pleasant to be hit by a hammer thrower's ball just before it was released. Or imagine a soccer ball positioned at the bottom of the arc of a park swing, and the force of the swinger's foot kicking it while swinging by. In a similar fashion, consider the centrifugal force generated by a weighted clubhead swinging at the end of a golfer's fully extended arms and dynamically constructed club shaft.

FIGURE 4-12   Completing the backswing.

2. Clearing the left side. An alternative approach for initiating the forward uncoiling action of the golf swing is to key on clearing the left side of the body out of the way in anticipation of the golf club swinging toward the target. Such a clearing action might be initiated by bumping the left hip toward the target as the first move of the forward swing. Another alternative initial move might be to slam the left heel down to the ground. Or the left hip might be simply turned out of the way as the whole body is directed toward facing the target. The effect of any of these left side maneuvers is to thrust the body's weight over to the left side with the anticipation of the arms, clubshaft, and clubhead following swiftly behind.

3. Driving with the right side. Still another approach for initiating the forward swing is to power through with the right side. More specifically, the first move of the forward swing is a turning action of the right hip toward the target. A feeling is generated that the right hip is driving past the ball with the clubhead again about to follow close behind.

Although teachers may argue over which approach for initiating the forward swing is best, effective swings using any of the above techniques are likely to look similar to the casual observer: An uncoiling action of the hips, the body's weight beginning its shift to

FIGURE 4-13   Initiating the forward swing.

the left side, and the club making an initial move toward the target with the wrists fully cocked. This doesn't mean that the debate is purely academic. From a mental standpoint, it may be very important which swing key the golfer is focusing on in producing an effective swing. That is, it may be important for some golfers to focus on the hands and club-head (Approach #1) as the guiding force in the forward move, whereas other golfers may benefit from focusing on the movement of the left or right sides of the body (Approaches #2 and #3) as the leading edge of the swing. Each golfer has to experiment to see which approach works for him or her.

The Hitting Area

Notice that as the hands move into the area of the swing arc where the ball is actually struck (Figure 4-14, left picture), the eyes are focused on the ball and the wrists are cocked and waiting to release all their power as the hands move over the ball. The subsequent release of energy into the ball happens so quickly that describing it or catch-

FIGURE 4-14   **The hitting area.**

ing it on film is virtually impossible. Suffice it to say that if the forward swing is initiated as described above, the action seen in the two pictures of Figure 4-14 will unfold automatically. Notice that after the ball has been struck (Figure 4-14, right picture), the head is still in position over the spot just vacated by the ball, and the arms are fully extended toward the target with the toe of the club pointing skyward. Observe also how the body's weight has shifted almost completely to the left side at this point in the swing.

The Follow Through

A powerful swing of the clubhead through the hitting area leads to a result of standing up fairly straight on the left leg, the hands high over the left shoulder, and the body facing the target (Figure 4-15). It's also at this point that the right shoulder will naturally bring the head up, allowing the body to turn fully toward the target. A conscious reminder to bring the head up is not necessary. Indeed, the greater challenge is in keeping the head down long enough to make solid contact with the ball (Figure 4-14).

FIGURE 4-15   The follow through.

**MENTAL SPOTLIGHT   Exhaling Hard When Ball's Hit Helps
Maximize Swing Potential**

There are certain principles common to many, if not all, sports. For example, seeing the hitting implement make contact with the object to be hit.

In golf, this involves the fundamental of "keeping your head down."

In baseball and tennis, it's following the ball all the way to the bat or the racquet. Successful football place-kickers are renowned for staring at the ground where they have just seen their foot make contact with the ball. Surely, polo, hockey and soccer players abide by this principle as well.

Another common principle would be following through toward your target. The golfer leads out with his hands and club toward the target. Baseball players do the same thing when trying to place the ball in a certain area of the field. Similarly, quarter-backs, free-throw shooters and bowlers make concentrated efforts to extend their arms and hands directly and smoothly toward their targets.

Recently, another element has impressed me as a possible common principle across a variety of sports. It has been popularized by tennis players, particularly the new generation. What I'm referring to is the emphatic "grunt" tennis players make at the point of contact with ball.

It's not the grunt that intrigues me so much as it is the exhaling that accompanies the grunt.

This focused purging of the lungs seems to be evident in other sports as well. Boxing is a prime example. At the moment of impact of a punch, boxers exhale emphatically. Similarly, football players do a lot of grunting and exhaling while blocking

continued

MENTAL SPOTLIGHT   *Continued*

on the line or during a tackle in the open field. Skiers put sharpness into their turns by punching down with the outside hand and simultaneously exhaling when their skis must swing around. Even exercisers doing sit-ups are advised to exhale as they move up from the supine position.

One notable exception, regarding exhaling at the point of impact, seems to be golf. How often have you heard a golfer grunt like a tennis player, or exhale so forcefully that mucous spews forth from various membranes, as often happens for boxers in the ring? If you ever have ringside seats at a boxing match, take an umbrella!

Of course, you haven't witnessed such activity in golf! Golf is much too refined. Admittedly, a golfer sometimes will overswing and produce a muffled groan. But, such an event normally requires an apology, lest one's playing partners chastise the golfer for "really trying to kill one." Noise, even the sound of effort, traditionally has not fit into golf.

With all due respect for tradition, if you want to add a few yards to your drives, a little grunt may be just the thing to provide that extra edge. I'll bet Mark Calcavecchia and Greg Norman grunt a bit when they make contact. In fact, Steve Thomas, the PGA Tour's 1988 long-driving statistics leader, told me recently that exhaling at impact was an ingredient of his powerful swing.

But, before totally embarrassing yourself, you may want a rationale for this grunting process. What can it possibly contribute to your performance? Let me propose three possible ways in which exhaling at the point of impact might contribute to more effective striking of the ball:

1. It creates focused power at the precise time you need it—the point of impact. The objective in swinging the club is to have a relaxed swing, saving your energy until impact with the ball.

At that point, energy is gathered and a firm thrust is unleashed on the ball, only to be relaxed again soon after impact. Exhaling accentuates muscle contraction at the critical moment. This is what boxers and karate masters do in generating tremendous power at the point of impact.

2. Concentrating on exhaling at the point of impact may eliminate other distractions and contribute to focusing on the ball at the point of impact. Remember the other common principle mentioned above—seeing the weapon make contact with the object to be struck.

3. Emphatic purging of the lungs—a forceful venting, not just a little whimper—creates an element of "abandon" at the point of impact. You let go, let things happen and don't hold back. You kind of go blank for a split-second, only to return in the next moment to see what happened. It creates an enthusiastic release, eliminating any lingering tentativeness in your swing. It contributes to an attitude of: Let's hit it, go find it and hit it again! It makes golf more aggressive, less worrisome and more fun.

Exhaling at the point of impact is, of course, not a cure for all golfing ailments. It is a refinement for maximizing the potential in an already sound swing. Tennis players don't grunt their way to stardom. They practice and learn the fundamentals of a good stroke, and they enhance that action with what might be termed the "power grunt."

Furthermore, this focused exhaling does not necessitate over-swinging, nor is it incompatible with a smooth swing. I believe the usefulness of the grunt extends even to chip shots, as they need just as decisive an action as the most powerful drives.

Lastly, the power grunt does not have to produce a lot of noise. What I do is empty my lungs about 90 percent just before my backswing, and, then, totally exhale the extra 10 percent when I make contact with the ball. This creates a forceful, but barely audible, "umph" at impact.

I'm sure it has gone unnoticed because no one has scolded me yet for ungentlemanly-like behavior on the golf course!

In summary, the general idea is to take your basically sound swing and accentuate the point of impact with a purging of the lungs. This should lead to less distraction, less tentativeness and an enthusiastic release of focused energy at the point of impact, where you need it most.

Remembering It All

All of the above is a detailed description of what happens during a golf swing. The ensuing challenge is to remember it all, particularly in the brief period of time it takes to make a swing. Somehow the memory task has to be simplified.

Psychologist George Miller (1956) established long ago that short-term memory capacity is limited to about seven bits of information. Telephone numbers nicely accommodate this capacity, but social security numbers can present a challenge. Short-term memory can be expanded somewhat by grouping things together into chunks. Even then, however, short-term memory is limited to approximately seven chunks of information.

Despite the interesting research of Professor Miller, there has probably never been a golfer who could remember seven bits or chunks of information during a two- or three-second golf swing. At best, one would probably do well to remember two to three things while actually swinging, and that may be pushing it. Consider the following suggestions for consolidating and simplifying the memory task in golf:

Note Cards

Write down on a note card important things to remember about the swing, and keep the note card in your golf bag or locker for quick review before playing. Nothing is more frustrating than taking six holes to remember a swing thought that was working so well the last time you were out.

Preshot Routine

Arrange in sequence the steps leading up to the actual swinging of the club. The sequence is a countdown that begins from behind the ball, looking down the target line. Once the line is determined, the ball is approached and the clubhead is placed behind the ball square to the target, followed by the proper alignment of feet, hips, and shoulders parallel to the target line. With the proper grip assumed and the body in position to begin the swing, another glance is made toward the target, the head is turned back toward the ball, and the swing is ready to go.

Note that the above preshot routine involves the more static considerations of a golf shot (i. e., grip, stance, alignment, body position). Once these factors are set in place, they do not require any further attention, and full focus can be directed toward the dynamics of the swing. In other words, once the countdown of the preshot routine has been completed, forget it and pay attention to only what is critical for blastoff.

Everyone develops a personal preshot routine. The important thing is that the routine, whatever it is, be repeated consistently every time a shot is made. If the preshot routine gets interrupted, stop and start all over again from the very beginning. One touring pro has been known to actually put his club back in the bag and take it out again if he becomes distracted during his preshot routine.

The preshot routine is not only a valuable memory device, it is also somewhat of a security blanket under pressure. It's something familiar that can be turned to in the heat of the action; it's a routine that will run off automatically when you are under stress.

Swing Thoughts

Once the preshot routine is completed and the actual swing is at hand, the only thing to be thinking about from this point on is the thought necessary to produce a proper swing. That swing thought might contain an upper limit of three components that would fit the 1–2–3 tempo of the golf swing—something as simple as "back-and-through." On the other hand, the swing thought might be slightly more complex and prescriptive. For example, if the golfer has trouble avoiding lateral body movement on the backswing, difficulty keeping the head down, and a tendency to stop before finishing high on the follow through, these flaws might be remedied with a three-component swing thought such as "still-down-high."

When really having trouble playing, revert to just one or two swing thoughts. The ones I always resort to in desperate times are to relax my hands and forearms, and see the contact between the club and the ball. Of course, during the swing, I simplify this by thinking "relax-and-contact."

The bottom line is that you can't consciously process very much at all during the actual swing, particularly those swings that occur during an actual round (as opposed to a practice round, or on the practice range). After going through the preshot routine, you just have to pull the trigger and let it happen. Don't wait too long to pull the trigger, either. It only takes a fraction of a second for a distracting thought to creep in between the completed preshot routine and the smooth beginning of the golf swing. The actual swing is kind of a leap of faith. You get ready (preshot routine), you get set (completion of the preshot routine), and you leap (smoothly begin the swing) without any definite assurance of what the ultimate outcome will be. Of course, the more you practice, the more confident you will become of a favorable outcome.

Monitor

Lastly, once a few reliable swing thoughts are discovered, don't take them for granted. It's easy to read them off a note card, say them during the swing, assume they are being faithfully executed, but actually be doing something quite different from what the swing thoughts suggest. Consider how easy it is to say, "keep your head down," while just as quickly lifting it up. Close self-monitoring is necessary lest a golfer slip into bad habits.

Expert golfers will often be seen, after a poor shot, stepping aside and making a few practice swings. Most certainly they are engaging in error correction, reviewing their swing thoughts before the next shot rather than during the next shot.

The key is to simplify the memory task to only a few unifying, overriding principles that can fit right into the tempo of the swing. The ultimate goal would be to get to the point where you don't have to think of much of anything during the swing. A grooved, well-practiced swing simply runs off automatically.

C h a p t e r **5**

The Key Shots in Golf

One of the elder statesmen of golf, Ben Hogan, reportedly said that if he were teaching someone to play golf under ideal conditions, he would start with the putter (the shortest club, which hits the shortest shots) and gradually work back to the driver (the longest club, which hits the longest shots). He thought the process would take about two years to complete, after which the student would only then be allowed on the course.

Naturally, this two-year plan is an ideal to which few novices would be dedicated enough to submit. Yet the sequence of learning that Hogan suggested holds considerable merit and will be followed in this chapter. Let's begin at the hole, therefore, with the putter, and gradually work back to the tee and the driver.

Putting

Putting consumes upwards of 40 percent of the strokes in a round of golf. That is nearly half the score, which suggests that putting should command at least half the attention in practicing and preparing to play. Billy Mayfair became an excellent putter, and the U.S. Amateur Champion, by devoting two hours of practice to putting for every one hour he spent on the driving range. Interestingly, he later found himself to be only an average putter on the pro tour, a situation he remedied with even greater dedication to putting practice.

Grip

The putter may be gripped in the traditional way as described in Chapter Four. It may also be gripped in various other ways, most of which are attempts to stabilize the left wrist so that it does not bend toward the hole during the follow through of the stroke (Figure 5-1). One common alternative for the putting grip is to reverse the overlap of the Var-

**MENTAL SPOTLIGHT   Golf's Beautiful Music Played
around the Greens**

There is a similarity between learning to play a musical instrument and learning to play a sport. I'm sure the similarity extends across many instruments and many sports, but I will reserve my comparison to the guitar and golf.

When you first learn to play the guitar, the task that seems so incredible is positioning the fingers of the left hand in various awkward positions to form chords on the neck of the guitar. The idea of quickly switching the fingers from one chord to another seems equally out of the question. On the other hand—literally and figuratively—the seemingly easiest part of playing the guitar is the right-hand strum across the strings at the base of the guitar. What could be easier than just dragging your fingers across six strings?

But as time goes by and you gain surprising facility with the chords of the left hand, there is an astounding realization of the myriad things you can do with the right hand. There are countless rhythms, finger picks, and combinations. You find that the demands on the right hand are much greater than those on the left, and that the right-hand component determines the true expertise of the virtuoso.

So it is with golf. When you first approach the game, it seems incredible how far accomplished players hit the ball, or that they even hit it at all with such a big swing. All you want to do is get the ball airborne and hit it a reasonable distance in the proper direction. The easier part of the game at first seems to be the short game, particularly putting. It would seem that anyone could roll a ball across a smooth surface into a little hole. And what's all the fuss about these little short putts? Similarly, the little pop-up shots with the wedge seem relatively easy.

Well, we all know that the opposite scenario soon emerges and seems to last forever. In due time, we find ourselves moving the ball off the tee, down the fairway, and into the vicinity of the green with surprising regularity. But, oh, the variety of wedge shots the game demands. And where did all these other chip shots come from? And who will ever learn how to really putt—I mean feel confident, once and for all, that the ball will continue to go in the hole with any kind of regularity? Even the excellent putters on tour have their ups and downs with putting.

Yes, just as with the haunting rhythms of the guitar, the beautiful music of golf is played around the greens. This is where the virtuosos preside, the classics endure, and great scores are produced.

don grip (which was discussed in Chapter 4), so that the forefinger of the left hand is covering the little finger of the right hand (Figure 5-2).

Stance

There are as many variations in stance as in grip when using the putter. The beginner, however, is best advised to start out with a square stance (see Chapter 4) with the feet about shoulder width apart and the toes of the shoes forming a line parallel to the target line. The ball should be positioned somewhere between mid-stance and the left foot, wherever it feels comfortable and encourages the hitting of the ball along the target line.

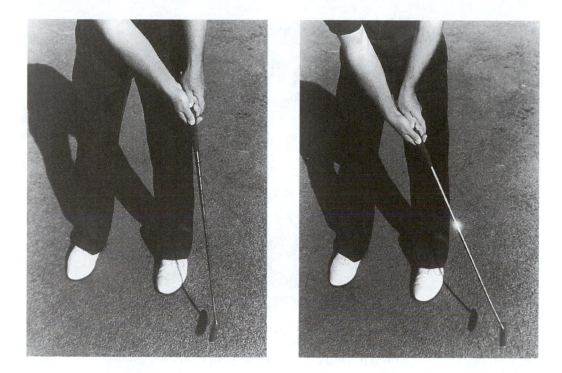

FIGURE 5-1   Correct and incorrect putter follow through. The correct procedure (left picture) shows the golfer stroking the ball to his left with a firm, straight formation of the left arm, wrist, and clubshaft. In contrast, the incorrect procedure (right picture) shows the golfer's left wrist breaking down (losing its firm straightness) and allowing the right wrist to "flip" the putterhead down the target line.

Body Position

Stand close enough to the ball so that the knees can be flexed and the body curled over, thereby positioning the eyes directly over the target line (the eyes might be right over the ball or a little behind it). To determine if your eyes are truly over the target line, hold a coin at the bridge of your nose and drop it. If it lands on the target line, then your eyes are correctly positioned. An image that may help to create this posture is to think of the whole body as a "question mark" curled over the ball (Figure 5-3).

Swing

Once the proper grip, stance, and body position have been assumed, the only thing remaining is to swing the putter. At a basic level, the fundamental principle attributed to Ernest Jones in Chapter Four applies to the putter as it does to other clubs—simply swing

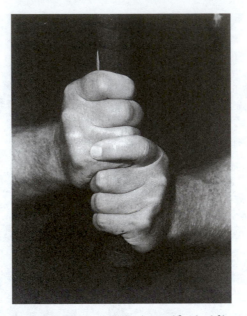

FIGURE 5-2   Reverse-overlap grip. With the golfer holding the club up so that the underside of the grip can be seen, notice how the forefinger of the left hand covers the little finger of the right hand.

FIGURE 5-3   Body position for putting. Notice how the golfer is curled over with his eyes directly over the ball and his body approximating somewhat the form of a question mark.

the clubhead toward the hole. A few caveats may be in order, however, to facilitate success with what is more commonly called the putting *stroke* (instead of *swing*).

1. Take the putterhead back only as short a distance as necessary to give the ball an accelerated stroke toward the hole. Acceleration means that the putterhead should be picking up speed as it moves through the ball toward the hole. The backstroke may be as short as three or four inches on one- to four-foot putts, or as long as 12 to 20 inches on putts covering 35–100 feet. But notice that even 20 inches is **not** a very long backstroke.

A common mistake of poor putters is to take the putterhead back too far and then try to slow it down as the putterhead approaches the ball. This deceleration results in considerable inconsistency, particularly with regards to the distance the ball travels. The proper technique is exactly the opposite of the above—a short backstroke with the putterhead picking up speed as it moves through the ball. An exaggerated image regarding this acceleration of the putterhead through the ball might be that of shuffleboard, where the disk is shoved with increasing speed down the court after no backstroke at all. Golf rules require at least a minimal backstroke, but keep it as short as possible on putts. An extended follow through toward the hole might also encourage acceleration.

2. Because the putting stroke calls for extreme precision, it is imperative during the backstroke and follow through to keep the head perfectly still. Any movement of the head can immediately throw the putt a fraction of an inch off line, which might result in a miss of a few feet by the time the ball rolls 35 feet to the hole. Even on a short putt, any slight movement of the head can result in the ball hitting the edge of the hole and "lipping out," as golfers say, instead of rolling dead center into the hole.

Keeping the head still during the golf swing is a challenge for everyone. When it comes to putting, the best assurance of keeping the head still is to plan on listening for the ball to drop into the hole, rather than on seeing the ball go into the hole. In order to get used to this, exaggerate the procedure at first. That is, stay down and listen for the entire roll of putts as long as even 20 to 30 feet. Just maintain the curled position over the ball's recently vacated resting spot, stare at the beautiful grass that had been under the ball, and wait to hear that even more beautiful sound of the ball dropping in the hole. Remember, if you look up, you are likely to see an undesirable result anyway!

Alignment

One last thing to take into account is that golf greens are not perfectly flat surfaces. Allowances have to be made for the slope of the green between the ball and the hole as well as any unusual bumps or undulations that might intervene.

The best way to assess the situation is from a position about 10–15 feet behind the ball. Stoop down low with the ball directly between you and the hole (Figure 5-4). Now, looking at the slope of the green, imagine how the ball will roll if it is stroked directly at the hole. If you visualize the ball drifting ten feet down the slope from the hole, then aim ten feet up the slope (Figure 5-5).

Once the target line has been determined, pick a spot about four to six inches in front of the ball along that line (e.g., a discolored blade of grass, an imperfection in the green, or an imaginary spot created by placing your putterhead in front of the ball) and align your putterhead, feet, hips, and shoulders with that spot. Then, simply take as short a back-

FIGURE 5-4   Player aligning putt.

stroke as necessary and accelerate the putterhead over that spot. Remember to keep the head still and be patient regarding seeing the result. Just listen for the ball to drop (Figure 5-5).

The Mental Side of Putting

Putting provides an interesting psychological paradox: Golfers often treat putting as if there were nothing to it. But, then, they nearly have an anxiety attack when the chips are down and they actually have to make one.

Consider the two halves of this paradox. Why would golfers think putting is so easy? Why would they think they can putt well with no practice other than a little warm-up before each round? Perhaps it's because putting was their first contact with the game. They played putt-putt golf as a child, and they hit balls around the house with a putter before they ever went to the course. When they finally did take up the game, putting was the first thing they were allowed to do. Therefore, putting must be easy since a child can do it, and because it's the first thing golfers are allowed to do when they take up golf. This is a wrong but understandable misconception, which is only added to by the pros making it look so easy on television (of course, after hours of practice).

Ironically, the anxiety surrounding putting may stem directly from this misconception about easiness. Why wouldn't one be anxious about failing at something that is so "easy"?

FIGURE 5-5   Player preparing to stroke the ball with a putter from the edge of an undulating green. Notice how his feet, and therefore the initial path of the ball, are
aligned toward the tree trunk in the middle of the picture, well left of the
flagstick (top picture). After the ball is stroked toward the tree trunk, observe how it curves from left to right toward the hole (bottom picture).

After all, if a child can do it, if it's the first thing you learn in golf, shouldn't you be ashamed of yourself for messing up such an easy task? Wrong, again. But try to convince your mind of that. Putting, indeed, provides an interesting set of psychological challenges, six of which will be explored next:

1. The first psychological challenge is to recognize and accept that putting is very difficult and that it will require a considerable amount of practice time. Meeting this challenge requires opening one's mind to the hard facts of the difficulty of putting. This shouldn't be too hard if records are kept of how many putts are taken per round and how much this number contributes to the overall score. Note also the putting performance of fellow golfers so as to appreciate the universal difficulty of putting. In addition, consider all the instructional articles, new techniques, and new equipment which are devoted to putting. Somebody must be struggling out there to consume all this material for what was formerly thought to be an easy dimension of the game.

Once convinced of the difficulty of putting, take responsibility for becoming a better putter. Responsibility is best understood by considering its opposite—blaming. A lot of things can be blamed for poor putting: rough green conditions, inadequate equipment, distractions, bad luck, and so on. In reality poor putters should blame only themselves. Then, and only then, can the serious task of developing the skill of putting begin. Remember: Putting is not luck, it's skill; and skill is each golfer's responsibility.

2. Being able to make four-foot putts consistently provides a tremendous advantage. Not only will fewer three-putt greens occur, but confidence about getting the ball in the hole in two shots from off the green will also be enhanced. This will take pressure off your short game, which should then take pressure off your long game and allow you to reach more greens in regulation (i.e., one shot for a par three, two shots for a par four, and three shots for a par five). So the whole game improves merely from learning how to make four footers!

The psychological challenge is to reduce the pressure and anxiety elicited by short putts, and this requires a little psychological trickery. That is, while the objective is to make every putt, if you keep saying, "I gotta make it, I gotta make it," so much pressure and anxiety can build that missing the putt becomes almost inevitable. Ironically, in order to make the putt, it is necessary to convince yourself that making it is actually secondary in importance. What becomes primary in importance is the action taken at the point of contact with the ball. In effect, you say to yourself: "If I can keep my head still and hit the ball firmly and squarely for the first six inches, then I have done my job. The remaining three and a half feet will take care of themselves."

In other words, don't take responsibility for getting the ball in the hole. Only take responsibility for the first six inches, leaving the rest of the putt to forces beyond your control. Do your job at the point of contact, recognize the limits of your control beyond that point, and the pressure and anxiety will be relieved.

3. Although short putts create considerable anxiety because of the feeling that every one should be made, longer putts can create an opposite mindset involving too little pressure and anxiety. That is, it's easy to think of nothing other than getting the ball close. Certainly it is true that if the putt is missed, it is desirable for the remaining putt to be close to the hole. But longer putts also need to be made every once in a while if a low score is ever to be achieved. Observe on TV the frequency with which the touring pros make 15- to

20-foot putts for birdies and pars. That's how they shoot those outrageously low scores, and that's what you have to do if you expect to shoot low scores.

The psychological challenge is to not be tentative. Develop a *make-it* mindset. Think of every putt as a putt to be made, an opportunity, a chance to score. Try to stroke even the very long putts into the hole. If getting the ball within a three-foot radius of the hole must be settled for, then don't be tentative about going for that three-foot radius. If you think "close" to the three-foot radius, then that is where the ball will likely end up—five to eight feet from the hole. That's too far for a comfortable short putt.

4. Sometimes you will have a hot streak with the putter for about 12 holes and begin thinking, "I'm due for a three putt." Or you may reach the seventeenth green having yet to miss a short putt only to talk yourself into missing a three footer by saying, "I can't go a full round without a miss." That reflects an expectation of failure and inconsistency that probably comes from having seen yourself fail to endure before.

The psychological challenge is to develop an expectation of success through an entire 18-hole round. Having previously seen yourself fail repeatedly, you now have to arrange a situation where you can see yourself succeed repeatedly—for 18 holes. Try this practice technique: Knock in 18 straight four footers from all angles around the hole before quitting practicing. If a putt is missed anywhere in the sequence, start over. Rest assured, when it gets down to putts number 17 and 18, the pressure will feel the same as it does on the course. And when 18 in a row are finally made, you will have seen for yourself that you can go an entire 18 holes without missing a short putt.

This same technique can be applied to practicing long putts. Simply require 18 long putts in a row without a three putt before ending the practice session.

Repeated practice using this method should change failure expectations into success expectations when it comes to enduring for 18 holes. Plenty of practice will also have been obtained with the psychological factors of pressure, frustration, and concentration, not to mention the grooving of the putting stroke that will have occurred.

5. Golfers are often seen slapping balls around on the putting green, never lining up a putt, leaving the little pins in the holes while they practice, and all the while yucking it up with their friends who are doing the same thing.

When these players get ready to hit their first "real" putts of the day, they receive a real shock. There are no little pins in the holes, they have to read the break without the benefit of multiple practice putts, and there isn't any joking when they're standing over the ball. The problem is that they didn't practice mentally or physically to prepare themselves for the real thing.

The psychological challenge here is to make practice as much like actual play as possible. During practice or warm-up, concentrate on the task at hand. Avoid conversations with other players; take the pins out of the holes and line up putts seriously; finish every practice hole, even the one footers that remain after a missed longer putt. If it is real golf for which you are preparing, then the warm-up practice has to be real, too.

6. Wildly different putters abound: long ones, bent ones, and ones with funny-shaped heads. New and varied techniques are just as plentiful: look at the hole, close one eye (even both eyes), putt cross-handed. Certainly there is merit in some of these, and some are likely to help in the short term. But none of them eliminate the need for the solid physical and mental fundamentals that lead to being a good putter.

The psychological challenge is to beware of heightened expectations based on fads. Build your game on solid fundamentals. If an innovation comes along that seems to work, go with it for a while, but don't be surprised if its effectiveness disappears as quickly as it appeared. Improvement based on fundamentals and hard work will endure, but sudden success based on novelty can be just as fleeting as the newness of the equipment or technique which created the success.

Chipping

The chip shot is used from just off the edge of the green where the grass is too long for putting. The chip is also appropriate at points up to about 30 yards from the green, where the distance from the ball to the edge of the green is less than the distance from the edge of the green to the hole. In general, the club of choice for the chip shot is one that propels the ball several feet onto the green, with the ball then rolling like a putt for the majority of the distance to the hole. Anything from a 6 iron to a wedge may achieve this objective under various circumstances. A little experimentation may be required from different positions around the green to determine the best club selections for you.

Grip

Because chipping requires a bit more wrist action than does putting, the standard Vardon overlapping grip (see Chapter 4) is the grip of choice, in contrast to the reverse overlapping grip recommended for putting.

Stance

The shallower angle and greater length of the shaft of the 7 or 8 iron, in contrast to the more upright angle and shorter shaft of the putter, will require standing a little farther away from the ball when chipping as compared to putting. An open stance (left foot drawn back from the target line a few inches) may also be desirable, enabling a better view of the hole and target line.

Body Position

Standing a little farther from the ball when chipping as compared to when putting, the body posture is slightly more upright and the eyes are not as much over the ball as is the case in putting (Figure 5-6).

The Swing

Despite these differences between chipping and putting, the more similar the techniques of the two shots, the simpler the short game. So, keep the backstroke short, accelerate through the ball, and, above all, keep the head very still. Again, just listen for the result.

FIGURE 5-6   Golfer chipping to shadowy green.

Pitching

Pitch shots are required out to about 60 yards from the green, where the distance from the ball to the edge of the green is greater than the distance from the edge of the green to the hole. Pitches differ from chip shots by flying higher and stopping sooner upon landing. In general, pitch shots are executed with the golfer's arsenal of wedges, although a club like an 8 iron might be used in situations where it is necessary to keep the ball low under some branches, and/or achieve a little extra roll after the ball lands on the green.

The pitch shot requires the precision of a chip shot, along with some of the power of a full shot (as described in Chapter 4). The grip, stance, and body position are those of a full shot, the only variation being that the stance might be slightly open (Figure 5-7).

Similar to the putt and chip shot, the distance the pitch shot travels is controlled by the length of the backswing. Golf's technical expert, Dave Pelz (1990), has distinguished nicely among the different backswings for executing the pitch shot. When addressing the ball, Pelz suggests thinking of the arms as hanging straight down at a 6 o'clock position. From this position, the arms can swing back to 7:30, 9:00, or 10:30 positions. If a swing with a consistent tempo is made through the ball to a full finish, the ball will travel consistently different distances for each backswing of differing length. It will be necessary to experiment to determine the precise distances that will be produced. The only caveats with

FIGURE 5-7   Golfer hitting pitch shot over mounds to nearby green.

the pitch shot are to cock the wrists completely on the backswing, follow through to a full finish, and keep the head still throughout the swing.

The Mental Side of Wedge Play

Because golf is not a game of perfection but rather one of surviving imperfection, good rounds are often built on avoiding disaster, in contrast to making one beautiful shot after another. To save par or bogey from what might have been a triple bogey can rival the thrill of making a traditional birdie.

Indeed, scrambling (i.e., getting in and out of trouble) seems to be very much in fashion these days, considering all the acclaim that accompanies some of the touring pros like Seve Ballesteros and Ben Crenshaw for their Herculean feats in the name of recovery from disaster. Ballesteros will never be forgotten for the successful shot he hit from a parking lot at a critical point in the British Open one year. In fact, the touring pros who are the statistical *leaders* regarding greens hit in regulation (i.e., one shot on a par three, two shots on a par four, and three shots on a par five) are only averaging about two thirds of the greens hit in regulation per round. Those are the leaders! Imagine what the average players are doing.

So, scrambling is in, it's here to stay, and golfers may as well learn how to do it well. And, just as with everything else in golf, there is a psychological side to scrambling. Since a great deal of scrambling is going to involve the wedge, the following will concentrate on that particular club.

1. All wedges are not created equal. There are so many wedges on the market today, it may require a consumer advocate to select the right one. At the very least, analyze your game regarding where the given club fits in, check all the lofts and varieties available, settle on a few clubs that seem to meet your need, and then let your final selection rest on the psychological considerations of look and feel. Considering the hazardous, pressurized, delicate situations encountered with this club, it is all the more important to feel as comfortable and confident as possible when looking at it and feeling it in your hands. So, pick the one that not only fits your game but also looks and feels good to you.

2. Cultivate pride in wedge play. Often players who came out on the short end of some friendly competition will complain that their opponent was "lucky," referring to the fact that the winner was very sharp with his short game on a given day. It is not luck. The old saying, "The more I practice, the luckier I get," is true. Don't feel guilty because of your short game. Never apologize for hard work and success. Practice, become expert with the wedge, and view each chance to use the wedge as an opportunity to demonstrate developing expertise. Relish the reputation of being the best wedge player in the area.

3. Keep the wedge handy. If there is one club that can be "messed around with" in a variety of circumstances, it is the wedge. It can't be done with the putter, where a green is required, or at least a carpet. You can't do it with the longer clubs where space free of obstacles is necessary to be able to fire away without fear of raining down golf balls on some unsuspecting property owner. But, the wedge, on the other hand, can be hit just about anywhere to just about anything. Some players waiting to tee off like to take out their wedges and hit a few shots to the tee marker. Shots can be hit to trees in the backyard. The wedge can be carried in the back of the car, allowing you to hit a few shots in the grass around the shopping mall while you're waiting for family members to finish shopping.

I'm reminded of a story about basketball star Pistol Pete Marovich. It's told that in his youth he seemed to have a basketball attached to his hand, the ball being his constant companion wherever he went. He would even bounce the ball outside the window of the car while riding along with his dad. The accuracy of this legend is secondary to what it suggests: To become expert with the wedge, make it a constant companion. Make the club an extension of the arms. Become so familiar with it that you can hit it in your sleep.

4. Play the percentages. Now that you've got the right club in the bag and have developed the appropriate expertise, an invaluable friend is available that will come to your aid in times of trouble. But don't abuse that friend. Don't let it be the club which is *always* reached for under any and all circumstances.

For example, the wedge can only hit the ball so far. So don't try to make the wedge do the work of an 8 or 9 iron. That's asking too much. When you're on the fringe or have a lot of green to work with, don't immediately grab the trusty wedge. Consider the putter, or a less lofted club that can roll the ball farther. Again, it may be asking too much of the wedge to loft the ball the perfect distance when such a trajectory is not necessary. Lastly, when an appeal to the wedge is necessary, hit it with the clubface square to the target whenever the shot will allow. The *cut shot* (covered later in the chapter) is usually going to be a lower percentage shot.

Think clearly. Don't turn a straightforward, easy shot into a delicate one simply because you want to use the old faithful wedge. If that friend is called on too often, particularly at inappropriate times, eventually it is bound to let you down.

5. Be precise. A lack of expertise with the wedge is likely to translate into a lack of confidence around the greens, with the ultimate result that the golfer just aims the ball in the general vicinity of the hole without focusing precisely on the target line to the hole itself. It's the "hit it and hope" syndrome.

In contrast, it's interesting how golfers sometimes pull off miracle shots around the eighteenth green when they have to knock a little approach shot into the hole to win the match. If they don't actually make the shot, they usually come much closer than would be the case under less pressurized circumstances. It seems that golfers become more focused in these "must do" situations, more focused on the target line to the hole.

Certainly common sense should be used in charging the hole, and aggressiveness tempered when there is danger of pitching the ball way past the hole or even off the green. However, in most cases it may be worthwhile entertaining the possibility of flying the ball to a precise spot where it will bounce a few times and then roll gently into the hole. Even if the objective is just to get it close, precision still comes into play by aiming precisely at the spot on the green that will result in the ball rolling into a three-foot circle around the hole.

6. Relax all the more with the wedge. In delicate situations around the green, any tension is likely to get in the way. Lighten up that grip and let the club do the work. Psychologically, it may be hard to accept that if you hit down, the ball will go up. But that's what the club was designed to do; and it will, if you relax and let it.

7. Visualize outcome. The wedge and the rest of the short game (i.e., chipping and putting) seem to lend themselves considerably to visualization. Occasionally, for whatever reason, a vivid image of a beautiful result comes over a golfer while preparing to hit an approach shot. Curiously, the actual outcome is often not far removed from the preshot image or vision.

The short game, with its fewer moveable parts, may avail itself to greater use of visualization of outcome than would be the case with longer shots. Fewer mechanics are involved and there is less potential for major mistakes, as can occur with a bigger swing. This frees the golfer up to focus on the target and the outcome, to conjure up beautiful visions of success, and to just relax and let it happen.

8. When in big trouble (sand, water, mounds, or deep rough) or when an obstacle such as a tree or bush must be negotiated, you are undoubtedly going to call on your old friend, the wedge. But don't forget that you have to do your part, too.

When trouble abounds, think about where you want to hit it, not where you don't want to hit it. Get a vivid image of success in your mind, get set over the ball, and don't look up again until you have seen the contact between the clubhead and the ball and replayed the successful image in your mind. Only then look up and be surprised if what you visualized hasn't really happened. This is how vividly visualization should be done, which is particularly difficult with all the distractions of a trouble shot.

Similar to a point made earlier, don't expect the wedge (or any other club for that matter) to be a miracle club that can always save you from tight spots the rest of your game is creating. The wedge can be a great asset, but if too much pressure is put on it, the wedge may let you down just like any other club. Don't get down on your wedge if the other parts of your game are creating all the trouble.

The Irons

Iron shots refer to full shots from the fairway or rough, using clubs ranging from the wedges and short irons (nine, eight, and seven) to the middle irons (six, five, and four) and long irons (three, two, and one). These shots will generally occur at distances of 70 to 200 yards or more from the green. The technique is the general swing described in Chapter Four, along with a few subtleties specific to these clubs:

1. There are two schools of thought on positioning the ball in the stance when hitting the irons. The simplest method is to position the ball out from the left heel in the direction your body is facing for every club in the bag. A slightly more complex method is to gradually move the ball back toward the middle of the stance when changing from the longer to the shorter irons. For example, the 2 iron would be positioned at the left heel, whereas the 9 iron and wedge would be positioned in the middle of the stance. The other irons would be positioned respectively between those two extremes (Figure 5-8).

For the beginner, playing all the shots at a position in the stance out from the left heel is recommended. Not only is this the simpler method, because it takes one variable out of the game (i.e., the ball position at the bottom of the swing arc), but it also encourages a forward weight shift to the left side if crisp contact with the ball is to be achieved.

FIGURE 5-8   Approximate ball position in stance for 2, 6, and 9 irons (right to left) if golfer chooses to adjust ball position in stance for various clubs.

MENTAL SPOTLIGHT   Don't Settle for a Big Target;
                       Golf Takes Intense Precision

Sometimes we unwittingly approach golf too generally instead of employing the precision golf requires.

This is obvious with the beginning golfer who takes a general swipe at the ball without the precision of technique that is required for a crisp shot. Similarly, the social golfer who generally applies the rules of the game as opposed to honoring the precision which the rules of golf demand.

But there are subtleties of precision which even the expert golfer can neglect. These subtleties involve focus and imagery, where generality can slip in before one knows it. Some examples follow:

1. A golfer will sometimes stand on the tee and gaze out at the fairway, rough, and other features that expand all the way to the green. He addresses the ball with this general image of terrain in mind, then just kind of hits it out there somewhere in the general direction of what is remembered.

In contrast to this general focus, precision would dictate picking a target at some point in the fairway and trying to hit the ball to it, just as one might do to a pin on a green.

2. When it comes to approach shots, there seems to be less of a problem with precision since the pin is an obvious target, or at least the fat of the green. But once inside 20 yards of the green, precise thinking may break down again. We can easily find ourselves hitting chip shots at the general vicinity of the hole, as opposed to precisely at the hole.

You may be able to identify with the beneficial effect of precise thinking on chip shots if you reflect back to a time when you needed to chip one in on the last hole to win or tie a match. Getting close was irrelevant—it had to go in. You concentrated intensely on the hole, not on the general vicinity of the hole, and either chipped it in or came a lot closer than you usually do. Why wait till the 18th to focus intensely on the hole?

3. Turning to long putts, I know there is the school of thought that suggests avoiding three putts by just getting the ball close, and I won't argue with that. But on the other hand, if you want to make the putt, you might enhance your chances by

aiming precisely at the hole. Again, it's amazing how close you can come on a long putt when you really need one for a last gasp win, and when you are really concentrating precisely on knocking it in.

But even if just getting it close is your objective, this does not negate the need for precision. The target simply changes from being the hole, to a three-foot radius around the hole. In other words, don't just hit the long putt at the hole hoping it will somehow end up close. Aim precisely at your three-foot target surrounding the hole.

4. On short putts, most golfers are finally thinking "hole." But now even "hole" may be too general. It might help to think "back of hole," particularly if one has trouble getting the ball firmly up to the hole. On the other hand, with very fast greens, one might want to cultivate the image of the ball falling precisely over the front edge of the cup. But whatever you think, there is no room for generality when it comes to short putts.

5. Nor is there room for generality when it comes to contact between the club and the ball. A golfer can too readily look at the ball, in general, as he addresses it. But when it comes to hitting the ball, he doesn't hit it, in general. He makes contact with the precise rear of the ball.

So fix your gaze precisely on the rear of the ball. As with a hammer and nail, you are much more likely to make crisp contact with the nail if you are looking precisely at the nail.

6. Lastly, don't just set the clubhead generally behind the ball. Address the ball at a precise point on the clubhead, be it with the driver, the 5-iron, or the putter. The putterhead position is of particular importance. Its position must allow you to hit the ball on the sweet spot of the putter, the spot where the putterhead won't wobble to one side or the other.

Some of the precision outlined above becomes semi-automatic with practice and experience. But golfers can never let their guards down completely, lest imprecision and sloppiness creep back into their games and diminish their effectiveness.

FIGURE 5-9   Golfer using old divot mark to align feet and clubface toward intended target. The proper alignment in this case appears to be just
right of the divot mark.

2. When a shot is being taken from close enough to the green to use an iron, getting
the ball close to the hole is a reasonable objective. So, be very precise about grip and stance,
and as Harvey Penick (1992) would say, "Take dead aim . . . and swing away" (p. 45).

To help with alignment, which can sometimes be difficult when looking at a distant
target, follow this procedure:

a. Stand several feet behind the ball, with the ball positioned precisely between you
and the target.

b. Pick a mark in the grass anywhere from a few inches to a few feet in front of the ball
and along the target line. The mark might be an old divot, a leaf, or a discolored blade of
grass. (Note: You can't place anything down in the grass as a marker; it has to already be
there.) Use this mark to align your clubface and then your feet as you take your stance (Figure 5-9).

c. Once having taken a stance, don't second-guess yourself if the aim doesn't look exactly correct when taking a final look at the target. Trust the procedure, maintain your
alignment with the mark in the grass, and swing away. With repeated good results, confidence in your calculated alignment will build.

The Fairway Woods

Fairway wood shots refer to full shots from the fairway or rough with any of the wood or metalwood clubs, including the driver when it is used without a tee. These shots generally advance the ball down the fairway until it gets within range for an iron shot. Sometimes the green may be reachable with a fairway wood. In any case, try to employ a similar amount of precision with these shots as was the case with the irons.

The ball is positioned in the stance out from the left heel similar to a 2 iron (Figure 5-8). The general swing described in Chapter Four applies here; however, the fairway wood swing may involve a bit more of a sweeping action versus hitting down into the ball as might be done with an iron. Simply sweep the club back and through like a big broom. Or consider Harvey Penick's image of swinging a grass sickle, simply clipping off the blades of grass under the ball with a smooth, flowing stroke.

There is no need to try to lift the ball into the air with the fairway woods or with any club, for that matter. The loft of the clubhead is designed to propel the ball into the air when it is properly swung through the ball. Any lifting action on the part of the golfer will only defeat the aerodynamics of the club.

The Driver

The driver is a special club, like the putter and wedge. *GOLF Magazine* (Frank, 1991) estimated that more than 80 percent of the shots in a round of golf are hit with the driver, putter, or wedge. So, just as the putter and wedge merit extra practice because of their important roles in the game, a little extra time spent in understanding the driver is also warranted.

The technique of swinging the driver is similar to that of swinging the fairway woods. The only adjustment might be to adjust the stance so that the ball is positioned an inch or two more forward toward the left toe, because the ball is now resting on a tee. Addressing the ball in this manner will encourage striking the ball just as the clubhead begins its upward movement. This combination of factors will provide a little more lift and clubhead speed at impact with the ball. If this adjustment creates a problem, however, it is perfectly fine to play the ball off the left heel, tee it low, and swing the clubhead just like a fairway wood.

The Mental Side of the Driver

The real challenge with the driver is mental. While it is a special club, it is not that special. Some players seem to attribute mystical properties to the driver, as if it were some supernatural implement that could save them from all their golfing woes. Others live in fear of the driver, as if it were a diabolical club that must be used only as a last resort. Actually, it's just another club that propels the ball a finite distance, needs to be aimed at a target, and is neither harder nor easier to use than any other club.

Nonetheless, the driver remains sacred to golfers. Who doesn't love to drive the ball, to go to the driving range, to hit the longest drive of the day? How could anyone improve on the concept of the drive?

Well, to begin with, the term *driver* itself conjures up unhealthy images. For some, it is like driving the most important nail of their lives with the biggest hammer they ever got their hands on. For others it is like driving a car, which requires steering the vehicle with a certain degree of hesitancy and caution that ensures safety. Still others might imagine driving off into the sunset, with visions of grandiosity and boundless horizons.

When it comes to driving the ball, neither nailing it, steering it, or driving off into the sunset will get the job done. The driver is not some special hammer, the club doesn't have a steering wheel, and the sunset can't be reached.

The best image for the driver is not one of driving the ball off the tee, but rather one of striking it smoothly down the fairway. It's a controlled shot with limitations that involve both direction and distance, as is the case with any other club or shot in golf.

With this caveat in mind, here are some psychological considerations for improving performance with the driver:

1. The initial drive off the first tee may set the stage for the golfer's attitude toward the driver for the rest of the round. So give special attention to that first drive when warming up on the practice range.

Of course, visualizing the first fairway while looking down the practice range may help, but I don't think that is helpful enough. It requires too much work imagining, and what ends up being imagined is too abstract to be effective.

A simpler and more effective technique is to practice the initial drive under circumstances that are as concrete and real as possible. To do this, don't randomly pick just any spot on the practice tee to hit from. Pick a specific spot that mimics the first hole. That is, if trees or out of bounds line the right side of the first fairway, then take a position on the range that has very real trees and/or a concrete boundary down the right side. This arrangement requires dealing with a real, concrete obstacle on the range that is similar to the one that is about to appear on the first hole. And it doesn't require any imagination.

At the end of the entire warm-up that has included hitting various clubs and shots, be sure to hit a few more drives of the kind that will be required on the first tee in the next few minutes. By doing this, the crucial first-tee swing thoughts will be firmly implanted in your mind.

2. On the first tee, you may be so anxious and eager to get the ball anywhere in play that you approach the drive in too general of a fashion. That is, you may find yourself thinking, "I just hope I can get it anywhere in the fairway or even in the short rough." Take a more precise approach. Don't just gaze into space, aiming in the general direction of the first fairway. Be precise: Pick a spot as a target and hit to it as if it were a flagstick on a green.

3. With the pre-shot routine complete, swing keys firmly in mind, and stance having been assumed, make one last review of your swing keys while waggling and taking a last look at the target. Then, hit it! Don't rush it or take a fast swing. Simply hit it before anything else can pop into your mind, such as, "I wonder where this is going to go?" or "I hope I don't look like a hacker here on the first tee!"

4. Once into the round and facing other driving holes, there may be a tendency to take on a distinct new attitude each time the driver is called for. After hitting a few good drives, it's easy to entertain delusions of grandeur. Even though you may suddenly feel like a gorilla, it is important to remember that you are still just a golfer with just a golf club in your hands.

Recall the images of nailing the ball or driving off into the sunset. Don't do that! Treat the driver like any other club. There is a limit to how far it can be hit. Just swing it smoothly like a 3 wood or any other club of limited potential.

A practice technique that might help in this regard is to hit 150-yard shots using the driver. Just tee the ball up and smoothly stroke out 150-yard tee shots of ideal trajectory but limited distance. Sometimes it is surprising how far the ball travels with such an easy swing.

5. On those rare occasions when you want to reach back for a little extra distance, just relax all the more and, if anything, take a bigger swing (i.e., increase the swing arc) rather than a harder swing. The power "grunt" might also be called upon (see Chapter 4, pages 38–39). That is, focus your energy on impact by exhaling emphatically at times of needing a little extra distance.

6. When pressure arises on treacherous driving holes that always have the potential to create trouble, feelings of anxiety, if not outright fear, are inevitable. Disastrous images are likely to be dancing faster than sugar plums through your head. At these critical times, which can make or break a round, stick with what you know best. If you naturally hit the ball low, for example, then play a low shot. Above all, don't try to hit an unfamiliar high-trajectory shot in this demanding situation.

7. Lastly, imagine needing the absolute best drive of your life, a circumstance which would undoubtedly be accompanied by a million distracting thoughts: "I want to see this ball go right up the middle. I don't want to see it going into the woods or into the trap. I want everybody watching to see what a good drive I can hit. Above all, I don't want to dribble the ball just off the front of the tee."

What do all these thoughts have in common? They involve *seeing* the results of the shot. There may be a desire to look up to see the results with the driver more than with any other club. After all, the driver is the big club. It's also the one which involves considerable uncertainty, stemming from the driver's greater potential for distance and lesser potential for accuracy. The driver generates more thrills than most clubs, thrills you don't want to miss seeing. It's the club for impressing others, and naturally you want to participate in seeing the grandeur of it all. Unfortunately, what is forgotten is that if you look up too soon, you are likely to see nothing but disaster. And, of course, everyone watching is going to see the same disaster unfold.

So, in a critical situation, the most important thing to remember is to keep your head down. Won't it be better to miss the first few seconds of the flight of the ball while everyone else is seeing a thing of beauty, rather than to look up and see right along with everybody else the entirety of a disastrous shot?

Specialty Shots

In following Ben Hogan's suggested learning sequence from hole to tee, a few important shots were left out because to introduce them earlier would have disrupted the systematic progression from the putter stroke to the full swing. Let's pick up those specialty shots now, as they will certainly be needed from time to time.

The Fade

At times it is necessary to curve a shot around some trees which interfere with taking a straight path to the target. A curve to the right is called a *fade*, and the shot requires nothing more than the normal swing with a slight adjustment in stance and grip.

In fading the ball, open the stance (as discussed in Chapter 4) so that your alignment is actually a little bit left of the target. Now, without changing the position of the hands which are presently aiming left of the target, allow the grip of the club to rotate slightly in the hands so that the clubface is pointed at the target. From this set-up, a normal swing will start the ball down the line to the left of the target formed by your toes, then spin it back to the right in flight toward the direction where the clubface was pointing at address. No changes in the swing are necessary. Just align your toes along the starting flight path to the left of the target, aim the clubface at the target, and take a normal swing (Figure 5-10).

FIGURE 5-10   Set-up for a fade. The golfer's feet are aimed to begin the ball's flight just to the left of the overhanging limbs in the foreground. The clubface is aimed more toward the center of the tree which should result in the ball curving to the right around the tree. A convenient image for the ball's flight in this picture is the cart path which curves from left to right around the tree.

The Draw

Drawing the ball refers to a shot that curves to the left, and the technique used is the mirror image of that used for the fade: Close the stance (as discussed in Chapter 4) so that your alignment is actually a little bit right of the target. Now, without changing the position of the hands which are presently aiming right of the target, allow the grip of the club to rotate slightly in the hands so that the clubface is pointed at the target. Again, take a normal swing. The ball should start down the line made by your toes to the right of the target and then spin around to the left in the direction the clubface was facing at address (Figure 5-11).

Uphill, Downhill, and Sidehill Shots

If the ball is resting on an uphill slope, simply play the ball more off the left foot, put your weight more onto the right foot so your body leans back a bit, and swing up the hill.

FIGURE 5-11   Set-up for a draw. The golfer's feet are aimed to begin the ball's flight to the right of the overhanging limbs in the foreground. The clubface is aimed more toward the center of the tree which should result in the ball curving to the left around the tree. A convenient image for the ball's flight in this picture is the cart path which curves from right to left around the tree.

Allow for the shot to move a little to the left of the target line, which is the natural tendency of the ball flight for an uphill shot.

If the ball is resting on a downhill slope, everything is the opposite. Play the ball off the right foot with more weight on the left foot so your body leans forward a bit, and swing down the hill. The ball is now likely to fly a bit right of the target line, so allow for this when aiming.

If the ball is resting on the side of a hill above your feet, simply move down the hill away from the ball and swing more around your body like a baseball swing. Allow for the ball to move left of the target line. If the ball is below your feet, move down the hill a bit closer to the ball and swing the club more upright (over your head), allowing for the ball to move right of the target line.

There are two common themes to all of these hill shots. The stance is always moved down the hill in relation to the ball, and your body and swing are always accommodating to the contour of the hill. It's kind of like pretending the whole world just leaned a certain way and your body and swing went with it. Once you and the world are leaning together, just take a normal swing.

Low Shot

Sometimes between tee and green, a *low shot* under some tree branches will be called for. Not to worry. Simply take a lower lofted club than would normally be used from that position (i.e., a 4 iron instead of an 8 iron), move the ball back in the stance toward the right foot, keep the clubface square to the hole (which will further decrease the loft of the club), and take a shorter backswing to hold down the distance the club would normally produce. The low shot, with its abbreviated backswing, is similar to the pitch shot, which was described earlier in this chapter.

When executing the low shot, as well as all the specialty shots, be sure to keep your head down. If you insist on seeing the ball go under the branch, you most assuredly won't! It is difficult not to take a premature peek under these uncertain circumstances. But it is imperative to stay down, gazing at where the ball was, even after it is gone. Otherwise, the shot is doomed to disaster.

The Cut Shot

This shot is used when it is necessary to get the ball up quickly over some obstacle, and then stop it quickly when it lands. The *cut shot* will generally be hit with one of the wedges, as these clubs are already the most lofted in the bag.

The technique for the cut shot is similar to another specialty shot—the fade—discussed previously. However, with the cut shot, the objective is not to hit a long, curving shot, but rather to hit a short, high shot.

As with the fade, open the stance so that the toes of the shoes are aligned to the left of the target and the ball is positioned well forward in the stance. The aim is now to the left of the target, so rotate the grip of the club in your hands so that the clubface is pointing back in the direction of the target. At this point, take a swing like a standard wedge shot discussed earlier in this chapter. Be sure to fully cock the wrists on the backswing, finish with a full follow through, and *keep your head down*. While the cut shot requires hitting decisively down on the ball, the ball ironically flies higher than normal with backspin on it, goes in the direction the clubface was aimed, and stops quickly when it hits the green (Figure 5-12).

The Sand Shot

The sand shot from a greenside bunker is a rather easy shot that many golfers make difficult. In order to realize the easiness of the shot, one must first understand the design of the sand wedge.

The sand wedge has a large flange, or bump, on the back of the clubhead. When the clubhead is laid on its back (as opposed to resting on its sole), the leading edge of the clubface is actually off the ground while the flange of the clubhead is actually in contact with the ground (Figure 5-13). The flange creates a bounce for the club as it passes through the sand, as opposed to the leading edge of the club digging into the sand.

FIGURE 5-12   Set up for cut shot. The golfer is electing to hit a cut shot because he has to hit the ball high over the sand bunker and stop it quickly by the flagstick which is just beyond the bunker. Notice the open stance and the clubface aimed in the direction of the target (left picture). Notice how the ball is positioned well forward in the stance, almost at a point out from the toe of the golfer's left shoe. Also, the club face is laid back almost flat on the ground (right picture).

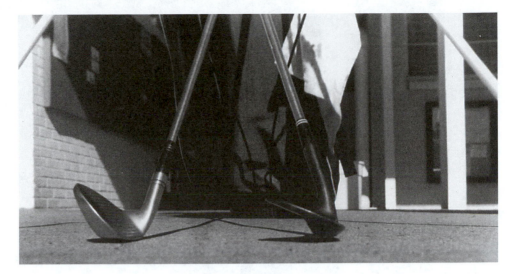

FIGURE 5-13   Comparison of soled sand wedge (left) and laid-back sand wedge (right). The soled sand wedge has the leading edge of clubface in contact with the ground. In contrast, when the sand wedge is laid back, the flange of the clubhead is in contact with the ground while the leading edge of the clubface is above the ground.

When the ball is sitting on top of the sand, the technique is the same as that described above for the cut shot. Simply open the stance, position the ball well forward in the stance, aim the clubface at the target by rotating the grip in your hands, and slide the clubhead under the ball to a full finish. Focus on a spot two inches behind the ball as the point where the clubhead is to enter the sand. Actually look at that spot rather than at the ball. When the club is swung, the bounce of the flange will move the clubhead through the sand on a shallow path, and the displaced sand will actually carry the ball to a soft landing on the green (Figure 5-14).

If the ball is buried in the sand, take basically the same swing. In this case, however, don't open the stance as much, and keep the clubface square to the target, allowing the leading edge of the sand wedge to dig into the sand an inch or two behind the ball. The ball should emerge with a bit more sand under it, on a lower trajectory, and with more roll.

If the ball is in sand some distance from the green (30 to 80 yards), or in a fairway bunker, hit a standard fairway shot with a couple of slight adjustments. First, move the ball back in the stance, as was done with the low shot described previously, which will encourage hitting the ball before the sand. Second, minimize lower body movement using mostly arms and hands in an effort to make solid contact with the ball. Take one longer club than normal, as a little distance might be lost due to the above adjustments.

FIGURE 5-14   A successful sand shot with the displaced sand carrying the ball
to a soft landing by the flagstick.

One last little wrinkle: You can't touch the sand with the clubhead before beginning
the backswing on the sandshot. That's right, the clubhead must hover above the sand,
the backswing beginning from a suspended position. No big problem, you'll get used
to it. In fact, Jack Nicklaus does this for virtually all of his shots—sand, fairway, or
green.

The Mental Side of Specialty Shots

Some of the specialty shots described above require considerable risk. For example, an intended low shot that is hit a little too high may catch a tree branch and bounce into
greater trouble than the original situation from which the shot was hit. Or a fade that
doesn't produce the intended curve from left to right may fly straight into the woods or a
water hazard.

Before committing to a particular specialty shot, consider whether the risk is worth
the potential benefit. For example, consider whether a successful shot will get the ball onto
the green in one stroke. If not, it's going to take two shots to get to the green from the ball's

MENTAL SPOTLIGHT   Perhaps It's Time for Golf to Re-examine Vernacular

In golf we have terms for shots that may create a disservice by conjuring up inappropriate images in our minds.

For example, consider the "explosion" or "blast" shot out of the sand. What comes to mind when you think of an explosion or a blast? You probably have images of a lot of energy and a lot of damage with a measure of fear thrown in. When you apply this imagery to a golf shot, it likely translates into swinging hard and blasting a cubic yard of sand out of the trap, with you in a state of considerable anxiety.

In reality, the sand shot can be a very delicate shot with very little sand involved. One can also develop considerable confidence and be quite relaxed with these shots, as is evidenced by the lack of fear the touring pros have regarding sand. They seem to hit sand shots with about the same degree of accuracy as they do long putts.

Indeed, if my recollection is correct, when Bob Tway hit his second shot into the trap on the last hole of his fabled PGA Championship victory, the professional analyst in the booth said that Bob would probably rather be in that trap than in a variety of other places. Little did the announcer know how prophetic he would turn out to be!

A second example of unhelpful imagery might be the "chip" shot, In everyday life, when we chip something like ice, wood, or glass, it is usually the result of a sharp, abbreviated blow to the object. In addition, when you chip something, it frequently occurs by accident—simply a chance event.

I think we often approach chip shots with a similar attitude. "Hit it and hope! Maybe by chance I'll get this close." We also tend to hack at them, as we would in trying to chip a block of ice, instead of hitting the shot smoothly and deliberately with a rhythm like that of other shots.

Next, how about the approach shot? Approaching, in our general usage of the word, suggests moving in the direction of something, getting nearer to the goal, but not actually being there. So what image does this suggest for the approach shot in golf? "Get it close, but not in the hole!" In fact, if it does go in the hole, it is usually quite a surprise to us because we were only thinking about getting somewhere in the vicinity of the hole.

Now contrast this scenario with the last time you had to sink an "approach" shot on the last hole to win or tie the match. Maybe it was just off the green, or even a very long putt. At the time you were not thinking of merely approaching the hole—you needed to knock it in. And lo and behold, if you didn't make it, you came a lot closer than would usually be the case. Could this be because you were not entertaining the image of "approaching" the hole, but instead were concentrating on the whole enchilada, putting it in the hole?

Last, but not least, let's consider the most sacred of all golfing cows, the drive. *THE DRIVE*, you say, what could possibly be wrong with that hallowed descriptor? After all, we all love to *DRIVE* the ball, to go to the *DRIVING* range, to hit our longest *DRIVE* of the day.

Well, we all know we have a different attitude about the golf swing when we get the driver in our hands. For some, it is like driving the most important nail in their lives with the biggest hammer they ever got their hands on. For others, it may be like driving a car, which requires steering the vehicle with a certain hesitancy and caution that ensures safety. Still others might conjure up an image of driving off into the sunset, with visions of grandiosity and boundless horizons that never end.

When it comes to driving the ball, neither nailing it, steering it or driving off into the sunset will get the job done. You haven't got some special hammer, the club doesn't have a steering wheel and the sunset can't be reached.

The image you need for the driver is not one of "driving" the ball off the tee but rather one of stroking it smoothly down the wide open fairway. It's a controlled shot with limitations that involve both direction and distance, just like with any other club or shot in golf.

Admittedly, golfers don't go around consciously entertaining these maladaptive images when they use the term explosion, blast, chip, approach and drive. But using these terms over a lifetime may result in subtle images becoming deeply rooted within us and working on us in ways that we are not even aware of. In any case, it certainly can't hurt to cultivate useful images that are more consistent with what the various shots in golf are really all about.

present location. Would it not be safer to play a less grandiose shot out of trouble and then make a standard approach to the green? In either case, the end result is going to be two strokes added to the score.

Specialty shots are great when they work and when the payoff is worth the risk. But don't be a foolish hero. Play the percentages, and your lower score will reveal your wisdom.

$$\textit{Chapter} \quad \textbf{6}$$

Practice: Make It Fun

Practice is considered to be work, whereas playing is considered to be fun. Notre Dame football coach, Lou Holtz, once said that he never found an athlete who didn't want to play—they just don't want to practice!

I think practice has been given a bad rap. Practice is as much fun as one makes it. Furthermore, if practice is also designed to be efficient and effective, it won't take as long as it might otherwise. I actually like to practice as much as I like to play. Let me tell you why:

1. Practice is relaxing. The pressure of an actual round is absent. Score is not an issue. Shots that I'm not happy with can be taken over. I can quit whenever I decide.

2. I'm successful. A goal is established that I usually accomplish. The goal might be the introduction of some new technique, or increased skill with a specific shot, or development of a different mental strategy. Whatever it is, I'm likely to be doing it reasonably well by the end of the session, which produces a feeling of accomplishment that doesn't always follow from a score-keeping round of golf.

3. Practice is fun. I make a game out of practice so that it has many of the fun elements of playing without some of the drawbacks of an actual round. Don't get me wrong—playing is fun, too. Practice and playing are just two different kinds of fun, and I like them both.

Practice is fun only if progress is being made. Therefore, the sections that follow will highlight how to get the most out of practice while still having fun in the process.

Lessons, Schools, and Other Instruction

Books do their best using words and pictures to describe the technique of the golf swing, but lessons are still important in applying these techniques to any individual golfer's particular style and talent. Someone who is knowledgeable about golf should be able to identify a number of capable teaching professionals in your area. Visit a few of them until you find one with whom you feel comfortable and who seems to understand your game. Then

71

MENTAL SPOTLIGHT   Key to Confidence Is Success, and Key to Success Is Practice

Many would say that the key to success is confidence. I would like to propose that the inverse is equally true, if not more so. That is, the key to confidence is success.

This is not a popular position to take, because it implies that there are no shortcuts. We would all like to find some gimmick that would quickly and automatically make us confident and produce a sudden metamorphosis in our game. But unfortunately, there are no miracle cures.

The only sure way to confidence is to succeed in situations where we would like to build confidence. If failure is all we see on the golf course, then we learn to associate the golf course with fear and doubt. On the other hand, if we regularly experience success when we play golf, then we come to associate golf with success, and this translates into confidence.

So that's all there is to it. Just go out and start succeeding!

But wait a minute—just how do you go out and start succeeding?

That leads us to another bitter pill to swallow. That is, success comes from practice. Among football coach Lou Holtz's repertoire of quips is the one that goes: "I've never found an athlete who didn't want to play; they just don't want to practice."

On the other hand, we hear stories about such pillars of confidence as Seve Ballesteros, who was re-portedly taking six to eight hours to play practice rounds for the Masters, because he was practicing shots from every conceivable position around the greens.

While the admonition to practice may not be the most welcome news, there is some consolation in that any lingering confusion about the basis for our lack of progress is eliminated, and we can quit wasting our time searching for "quick fixes."

It's kind of like having some mysterious physical ailment and being afraid to go and find out it's just as bad as you thought it was. But ironically, it's a relief to find that out for certain, even if the news is bad. The relief comes from the realization that you can now get started on the productive route of doing something about your problem.

Of course, the remedy for your golfing woes is a systematic program of practice that is consistent with psychological principles of learning.

So as you start this golf season, make a realistic plan regarding practice and stick with it. Keep a record of your performance (and remember that score is only one measure of performance) and see if you don't notice some improvement over the season.

Look for small, steady gains.

You may never feel confident that you can go out and break par. But at least you can build your confidence in your ability to achieve the realistic goals toward which your practice program is targeted.

stick with him or her for at least a while, so as not to get confused with too many different approaches to the golf swing.

Golf schools are another option that provide an intense, concentrated regimen of learning involving all phases of the game. Golf schools are often located at resorts, can last from a few days to a week, and may include everything from private lessons and personalized videotaping to group clinics and tournaments. Schools can be an enjoyable part of a vacation. But I still believe that private lessons in the golfer's hometown, spread out over a period of time with plenty of intervening practice, are more economical and more productive in the long run.

Of course, golf books and magazines remain the most economical source of instruction in golf. Many good ideas can be garnered from the written word of golf's gurus. Just don't try to experiment with everything new that comes along, or confusion may set in along with disruption of your basic practice program. If some little tip is discovered that can easily be incorporated into the basic swing, give it a try. It may, indeed, provide the extra edge that has been lacking. Just be careful not to tamper too much; and any experimenting you do undertake should be done during practice rather than in the middle of a competitive round.

Prepare Mentally for Lessons

Mental preparation is as important as physical preparation in getting the most out of the golf instruction available. A good thought as lessons are begun is that "you learn what you practice." Quite simple and obvious at first glance, but there are several subtleties to this principle that should be highlighted:

Practice Requires Repetition

What is learned directly from lessons, clinics, and instructional schools is quite limited. More precisely, a pro shows you *what* to learn during a lesson. The actual learning of the technique takes place during the hours of personal practice invested following the lesson. To take a lesson and not practice afterwards is like buying a product and not using it. Consequently, in planning mentally for spring training, be sure to allow time for ample practice between lessons.

Practice Takes Time

Therefore, learning also takes time. Be patient; don't expect miracles overnight. Instead, look for gradual improvement over the course of the season. Keeping records and charting various performance measures may help in identifying small improvements that might otherwise go unnoticed. Remember that small, gradual gains add up to major improvements in the long haul.

Practice Must Be Done Carefully

Since you learn whatever you practice, be sure that you are actually practicing what you need to learn. This, too, may sound elementary, at first. Yet it is amazingly easy to think you are doing something correctly, only to find out later that all along you have been practicing and learning some mistake. A classic example of this is when practice is done carelessly. Carelessness is practiced and learned instead of carefulness, which is what is needed on the golf course.

Therefore, when it comes to getting the most out of lessons, concentrate on precisely proper technique, and practice it carefully and diligently afterwards. Above all, don't inadvertently waste a lot of time practicing and learning bad habits.

MENTAL SPOTLIGHT   Golf Is *Not* 90 Percent Mental

Despite what you've heard, the game of golf is *not* 90 percent mental. This may sound surprising coming from a sports psychologist. But the alleged 90 percent estimate has put too much pressure on the mental side of the game and let the physical side off the hook.

The fact is that many golfers haven't taken the time to learn the physical fundamentals of the game. When things go wrong, psychology gets the rap. Why? Because they think golf is 90 percent mental!

Here's a good example: "I could putt great if I could just get my nerves under control." How many times have you heard that? If this golfer had spent adequate time building and practicing a solid stroke, he might not have quite as much trouble with his nerves.

Don't get me wrong—I'm not saying solid physical fundamentals make the mental side obsolete. I am saying that you can't work on one without the other. You can spend hours working on visualizing the perfect shot, but you're still going to miss the fairway if you have a faulty grip.

That's why you should never view the mental side as the cure to all your game's ills. Do you really want to place all that blame on your psychological make-up, your "self"? It seems a bit unhealthy to believe that the only reason your game is weak is that your head is messed up.

If forced to make a realistic equation, I would say that golf is about 50 percent mental, 50 percent physical. There are constant psychological challenges in trying to relax over the ball, finding an appropriate swing thought, controlling your emotions, visualizing effectively and building confidence in the face of all this stress. But there are comparable physical challenges: lining up correctly, shifting your weight properly, negotiating difficult recovery shots, not to mention putting.

The question is, how do you develop the mental side of your game along with the physical? The answer is one you've heard before: Practice, practice, practice.

But truly effective practice—the kind that develops both sides of your game—doesn't mean beating balls or knocking a few putts around the putting green. Here are a few things to keep "in mind" when you practice:

Go the whole nine yards. Whether you're at the range or on the putting green, make each shot count, as you would on the course. Pay attention to your preshot routine, visualizing each shot and working on feeling relaxed over the ball. Most important, do this on every shot you hit. That way, you'll be developing and grooving a mental routine as you work on the physical.

Find "the key." As you practice, search for the swing key that you can latch onto and concentrate on throughout the upcoming round. Make that a major goal of each practice session; don't keep stubbornly whacking away, expecting your swing to eventually iron itself out. Be aware of what you're thinking on each swing until you find a thought that leads to successful shots.

Finish strong. A major component of a sound mental game is confidence, which, unfortunately, eludes many golfers of all levels. Confidence doesn't just happen—it comes with success. So make sure you finish your practice session well. Suppose, for example, that you're working on straightening out your occasionally errant driver, but you're only seeing mixed results. Don't let frustration be the legacy of this practice session. End your session when you have hit your drives on the good side of those mixed results. That way, you'll retain a favorable image of success between practice sessions, which may be a step in the direction of conquering your driver the next time out.

You might feel it will take twice as much work to improve, because not only do you have to concentrate on physical fundamentals, but you must train your mind at the same time. Don't be discouraged. Training your mind and body at the same time doesn't mean more practice; just practice with a well-planned purpose.

By Thomas N. Dorsel, *GOLF Magazine* (August, 1991). Copyright © 1992, 1993 by *GOLF Magazine*.

Motivation to Practice

The following are some suggestions for getting yourself to practice between lessons:

Make Practice Convenient

Keep a few clubs in the car so you can conveniently stop at the driving range on the way home from work. This beats going home, gathering up equipment, and coming back to the driving range—a major ordeal which is likely to be avoided.

If the children are always dropped off for swimming lessons on Saturday at 10 a.m., start using the waiting time as regular practice time. Similarly, if you happen to come across a little free time during your travels, a wedge and a few balls kept in the car can always be used to practice chip shots on the nearest patch of grass. Of course, a putter at the office and a nice smooth carpet can't hurt the mechanics of the putting stroke either.

Keep Records

Pioneering sport psychologist, Peter Cranford (1961), suggested the enjoyment in record keeping. He noted the pleasure in posting scores, striking averages, and noticing trends. Every stroke becomes important, there is something to shoot for every time you go out, and you have a permanent golfing partner—yourself.

Keep Alternative Scores

Even when the 18-hole scores are frustrating you to death, there are other scores that can be tallied to keep motivation alive. For example, play a *match against par*: Every time a hole is parred, you win the hole (birdies count for two); bogeys and above count as a win for the course. If you are a bogey shooter, simply adjust the system a notch higher so that you can be competitive.

Another alternative score to consider is a *good shot* score. You get a point each time a shot is hit using the correct technique, regardless of the outcome of the shot. For example, if keeping the head still is the practice objective of the day, you get the point each time that objective is accomplished, no matter how the shot turns out.

In addition to using alternative scores as a practice technique, keeping alternative scores during regular rounds can also be a good idea in maintaining motivation after those occasional back-to-back triple bogeys on the front nine.

Stop Practicing While It Is Still Enjoyable

If a reader puts down a book at an exciting part, she is more likely to return to it eagerly than if she pauses at some routine breaking point such as the end of a chapter. It's the same with golf. Quit while the practice is fun and some good shots are being hit. Then you'll be eager to come back to see if you can do it again.

Practice the Whole Game

It is tempting to dissect the game into its parts and focus on only one part at a time when practicing. Indeed, when first building one's game from putter to driver, as discussed in Chapter Five, a dissected approach may be well-advised. Practice chipping and putting greens and the driving range are well suited for learning the basic swing, for practicing certain specific elements of the game, and for refining the swing over the course of a golf career.

But once the basic strokes are learned and golf is being played regularly, a golfer should resist dissecting the game too much. The reality of golf is that during actual play, drives, approach shots, pitches, chips, sand shots, long putts, and short putts all have to be hit in succession, rarely hitting two shots of the same kind in a row. In addition, shots are hit from varied terrain, to include fairway, rough, sand, hardpan, uphill, downhill, and sidehill lies. To complicate things further, club selection, strategy, and score keeping are involved. And don't forget the mental side of each shot, which has to be handled simultaneously with the physical. In other words, *playing* golf is complex; and to become proficient at it, you have to *practice* the same game that is to be played, in all its complexity.

The implementation of an integrative, complex approach to practice is not without problems. It will have to take place on the course, the only place that will provide all the demands of the game. But practice on the course is sure to meet with resistance from other golfers and management. Although this is understandable, it is somewhat disconcerting considering that golf is the only game that is not practiced on the same or similar field as that on which it is played. Baseball, basketball, and football players are not kept from practicing on their respective fields. Bowlers don't practice in the driveway; tennis players don't practice without a net. Yet golfers are relegated to the driving range, which is anything but complex; or to some unimaginative chipping/putting green, which hardly mimics the demands of the short game on the course.

Still, it is understandable that practice on the golf course is discouraged, especially during peak playing time, or on courses so finely manicured that one is hesitant to even walk on them. If a golfer wants to have any chance of practicing on the course, therefore, prudence will have to be exercised in the following ways: (1) Practice at non-peak playing times (early morning, late evening, off season). (2) Don't overdo it by hitting too many shots from any one place, which would damage the course as well as make practicing on the course more obvious. (3) Be as inconspicuous as possible, not broadcasting the fact that you are practicing on the course. When other players appear, let them play through without hesitation, exercising perfect etiquette and not giving anyone reason to complain. (4) Go the extra mile in terms of course maintenance. Because practice may put a little extra wear and tear on the course, repair not only your own damage, but everything in sight (i.e., divots, ball marks, unraked sand traps). The motto should be that courses are not hurt by use but by abuse, and you are rectifying any abuse you see. If anybody does complain, you can assert that contrary to hurting the course, you ought to be given the "junior greens superintendent" award for all the volunteer maintenance you provide. (5) As a last resort, if you are actually forbidden from practicing on the course, seek out another course that is hard up for players. Management at such a course is likely to be less concerned about your activities, and they will be appreciative just to have your patronage.

Having managed to produce a situation where practice on the course is possible, the problems are not over. Practicing on the course poses difficulties regarding the efficient use of time. Specifically, too much time may be wasted walking, when more practice shots could be taken. Another side to this coin, however, is that time spent walking may not be wasted after all. It allows you time to practice certain components of the game that are often neglected during practice on the driving range, such as strategy and club selection. The actual tempo at which the game is played is also experienced. Walking forces one to slow down and distribute practice, something that is rarely done on the driving range where golfers fire shots in rapid succession, like a machine gun. Finally, the protracted investment of time and effort connected with walking between shots may have the added advantage of making each shot more important, as opposed to being just another ball on the driving range. Indeed, one shot practiced carefully is likely to be worth more than numerous shots practiced carelessly.

Mastery Practice

Having hopefully convinced you that practice on the course is important, that it can be done with a bit of ingenuity, and that even its drawbacks have their beneficial aspects, it is time to introduce the most effective, efficient, and fun way to practice on the course—*mastery practice* (Dorsel, 1978; Dorsel & Salinsky, 1990).

Mastery practice involves playing the course as if playing a regular round, with the added requirement of mastering each shot along the way. Mastering each shot means taking each shot over until it is hit correctly—be it on the first, second, third, or fourth attempt. Once the successful shot is made, no more extra shots are taken and the golfer goes to where that final shot lies and repeats the process. (Note that this is different from hitting four shots and choosing the best one. With mastery practice, extra shots are stopped when the successful one has been hit.) Of course, this procedure leads to unbelievably low-scoring rounds relative to the golfer's normal level of play, and, in fact, would be considered cheating if it were done under playing conditions. But this is not play, it is practice; and the measure of interest is not a spectacular score but rather how many extra practice shots it takes to achieve that score (Figure 6-1).

In addition to the fun of a low score, mastery practice offers a number of special advantages over other practice techniques:

1. There are no absolute standards for mastery practice. The successful shot one requires from a given point on the course can vary according to one's ability and/or the particular playing conditions one faces. For example, a beginner might be very happy to hit shots that will achieve two over par on every hole, whereas a pro might strive for one under par on every hole. Similarly, on a wet and windy day, one might alter the standards a bit to allow for the less than desirable conditions; or on a very difficult course, the golfer might be satisfied with bogeys on some holes in lieu of the usual expectation of par on every hole. In other words, mastery practice lends itself to individual tailoring to the caliber of player and the particular demands of the playing situation.

FIGURE 6-1   Golfer hitting a fourth chip shot toward the hole during a mastery practice session.

2. Practice occurs in the context of the actual game, doing exactly what is trying to be learned. That is, practice involves being on the course, hitting a variety of shots from varied lies, walking, thinking, and even keeping score. All of these similarities should facilitate generalization to the situation of playing an actual round.

At the same time, more shots are being hit than would normally occur during a traditional round, an advantage usually obtained only on the driving range. Mastery practice, therefore, provides a nice compromise between the advantages found in playing and the advantages found on the driving range.

3. How much practice occurs, and exactly what is practiced, are both regulated by the current level of play. That is, if a player's performance is presently poor, practice is automatically increased because more extra shots are required to obtain successful ones. If the driver is being hit poorly, extra drives will be called for. On the other hand, if the sand game is going well, there won't be as many extra shots taken from the bunkers. In other words, attention is focused on the clubs that are most in need of practice.

Mastery practice is comparable to a thermostat in a house. When rooms (or clubs) get cold, the heat (or practice) kicks into action. When the rooms (or clubs) warm up, the heat (or practice) backs off.

4. With continued mastery practice, the outcome should gradually be shaped toward approximating the perfect round. That is, as one's ability improves through mastery practice,

fewer extra shots are required. If this successful scenario were pushed to the extreme with no extra shots being required, then the perfect round of golf would be executed. Although it is highly unlikely that anyone will ever shoot the perfect round, the closer perfection can be approximated through mastery practice, the better the indication of improving skills.

5. Relaxation is conditioned to the context of the golf course. Unsuccessful shots lead to anger, frustration, and tension, and anything that precedes or signals the likelihood of unsuccessful shots will also come to elicit tension.

Imagine this scenario: A golfer has a history of driving to the golf course, getting her clubs out of the trunk, walking to the first tee, hitting a poor drive, and experiencing anger, frustration, and tension as a result. After many repetitions of this sequence, she begins to find tension building up as she drives to the course and approaches the first tee, even before hitting any bad shots. This anticipatory tension makes it more likely she will hit a bad shot, which, in circular fashion, makes it more likely she'll experience even greater tension the next time she approaches the course.

Now imagine the opposite scenario: The same golfer drives to the course, approaches the first tee, but now hits a good shot, with peace and relaxation as the result. After many repetitions of this sequence, she experiences an anticipatory state of calm as she approaches the course. This relaxed state enhances the likelihood of hitting a good shot, which, in circular fashion, encourages even greater relaxation the next time she heads for the course.

As discussed in Chapter Four, it is imperative to relax on the golf course in order to efficiently execute the golf swing. Mastery practice is a way to encourage relaxation by reducing unsuccessful experiences that lead to tension and increasing successful experiences that lead to relaxation. A new state of calm is substituted for a previous state of anger, frustration, and tension. A feedback loop is created that encourages even greater relaxation the more practice occurs.

6. Mastery practice provides you with the ideal model to imitate—yourself. Psychologist Albert Bandura (1969), in describing learning through imitation, said people are more likely to imitate models who are (a) similar to themselves, and (b) successful. The ideal model for learning golf, then, would be someone who resembled the learner exactly and who was also hitting successful shots.

Voila! Mastery practice does it again. Golfers see none other than themselves (their perfect resemblance) hitting beautifully successful shots. To put it slightly differently, learners see that they have it within themselves to hit every shot necessary for an excellent, if not perfect, round. Thereafter, the golfers know they have the potential to perform successfully on any hole on the course.

7. Pressure can be applied by keeping records of practice performance. Specifically, after each session chart the number of extra attempts necessary to shoot the target score.

Mastery practice reverses the constants and variables in golf. That is, the usual variable in golf is the score, changing from hole to hole and round to round, whereas the number of attempts from each point on the course remains constant (i.e., one attempt). With mastery practice, however, the score becomes constant (i.e., pars on every hole), whereas the number of attempts from each point on the course varies.

By keeping records of the number of extra attempts needed, pressure is applied to hit good shots as soon as possible. An increasingly lower extra-shot count on the chart will, in turn, reflect favorable progress.

MENTAL SPOTLIGHT   Don't Make Hard Game Harder:
Nine Rules Reduce Failure Factors

Practice will always be the most important ingredient for success. But there is something else you can do that will enhance your chances of success—eliminate factors that might be expected to lead to failure.

Dr. Peter Cranford, a pioneer in applying psychology to golf, offers nine suggestions to help reduce your likelihood of failure:

1. Avoid playing too many different sports. If you divide your practice time among many sports, you run the risk of devoting too little time to any one of them. To paraphrase an old saying, you may make a reasonable showing in several sports but be a true success in none. This is not as confidence-building nor as personally satisfying as being recognized as truly competent in one given sport.

2. Don't play with better players all of the time. It is going to be difficult to succeed in terms of winning matches if you constantly play with better players.

3. Avoid playing with people who make you anxious. If you are tense, embarrassed, or feeling a need to impress someone, you are not likely to play your normal game. This is likely to lead to failure.

4. Don't play when you aren't feeling well or are preoccupied with something else. If you are not able to concentrate on golf because you are concentrating on other matters, your performance in golf is likely to suffer.

5. Stop playing when you are getting nowhere. The mere fact that you are getting nowhere indicates that you are already failing, and the frustration that is likely to occur from confronting constant failure can only increase the likelihood of further failure. Take a break, take a lesson, but don't keep frustrating yourself by doing the same fruitless thing over and over and getting nowhere. If there is one rule that holds in life, as well as in golf, it is: If you are doing something and it is not working—quit doing it and try something different.

6. Beware attempting shots that you "don't have in your bag." If you haven't practiced a given shot, then you haven't learned it. And when you try something that you haven't learned, you are likely to fail. Golf legend Ben Hogan allegedly practiced new, experimental shots for months and months before ever using them in an actual round of serious golf.

7. Don't give overly generous handicaps to poorer golfers or refuse adequate handicaps from better golfers. If you do either, you are likely to fail because you are stacking the cards against yourself.

8. Be careful about increasing betting when you are down. If you are down in the match, you are already in the process of failing. To increase the betting might only compound the problem by increasing your motivation. Motivation does not redirect behavior; it simply energizes it in whatever direction it is already going. If you are already failing, playing poorly, and losing a little money, you don't want to energize that failure, play worse, and lose a lot of money.

9. Beware of accepting "gimmes." While such so-called gifts may lead to immediate "success," it is a tainted success. More importantly, accepting gimmes deprives you of practice on short putts, which may subsequently lead to failure when the chips are down and you have to make the short ones.

In conclusion, enhance your success via practice, and reduce your failure by not unduly penalizing yourself or making things harder on yourself than golf already mandates. Work hard to develop your game, but then give yourself a fair chance to succeed.

8. There are a few other notes of caution regarding the use of mastery practice:

a. Be reminded that mastery practice does not involve hitting five or ten shots and then choosing the best. The essence of mastery practice lies in attempting shots only until a good one is hit. And it is desirable to hit a good one as soon as possible, ideally on the first attempt.

b. Be demanding regarding what is accepted as a good shot so as to ensure that enough overall practice is achieved. That is, don't make the task so easy that the first attempt is regularly acceptable. Certainly, it will sometimes happen that a good shot occurs on the first attempt, and you hope it will happen more often as mastery practice continues. But if a level of accomplishment sufficient enough to lead to improvement is demanded, more than one or two attempts are likely to be required to achieve an acceptable shot.

c. Mastery practice ideally involves taking as many extra attempts as are necessary to master the shot at hand, but a limit of four total shots from any one point on the course may be practical. That is, if a successful shot is not hit by the fourth attempt, play the fourth shot no matter what the outcome. This limitation is likely to keep the practice session moving at a reasonable pace, distribute practice more evenly over the whole course and over various shots, and add a bit of pressure to the situation because of being stuck with a potentially poor fourth shot if a good shot is not achieved earlier in the sequence of extra attempts.

d. Be sure to play at least one round of traditional golf to every two mastery practice rounds. Otherwise, dependency on extra shots and reduction of generalization to actual play might occur. *Practice* enough to build skill, confidence, and relaxation; but *play* enough so that the skill, confidence, and relaxation carry over to actual rounds and not be limited to merely practice sessions.

Imaginative Driving-Range Practice

When mastery practice is not possible or practical, imaginative driving-range practice might be a second-best alternative. This approach involves practicing on the driving

FIGURE 6-2   Golfer positioning himself on the driving range to practice shots that involve a line of trees to his right.

range but making driving-range practice as much like playing conditions as possible. For example, have a course in mind and play through that course in your imagination, working through the clubs as would be required in playing that course. Aim at targets that approximate those on the course. Hit down the right tree line of the range if there is trouble to the right on a given shot on the imaginary course (Figure 6-2). Consider including trips to the chipping and putting greens at those points in the practice routine where chips and putts are called for. Require mastery with each shot, taking each one over until it is properly executed. A bonus with this type of practice is that one can take as many extra shots as he or she wants on the driving range.

Although a viable alternative to mastery practice, imaginative driving-range practice is a second choice for two reasons: (1) It requires double duty: *Imagining* situations as well as *executing* the shots. With mastery practice, imagining situations is not necessary, because the concrete demands of the course are present. Execution is all that is necessary. (2) As innovative as one might be, the driving range cannot possibly present the variety of lies, obstacles, and targets which are automatically generated on the course under mastery practice conditions.

Practice under All Conceivable Conditions

Hills, water, and trees are everpresent on the golf course. Tournaments aren't cancelled when gale-force winds start blowing. Play can often proceed through a stubborn, cold drizzle. If play may occur under these various conditions, then some time must also be devoted to practicing under these conditions (Figure 6-3).

It has been said that when the Texas winds started to blow, Ben Hogan would go out on the course and play four balls for extra practice under those challenging, Texas conditions. Incidentally, Ben must have seen some value in practicing on the course, if this legend is true.

Another issue related to practicing under playing conditions is carpet putting, be it at home or on a putt-putt course. Cranford (1961) suggested that carpet putting might be useful in standardizing the grip, stance, and stroke so that it will become easily repetitive. Carpet putting might also be of value with short, straight putts that can be rammed into the hole. But when it comes to learning actual green putting with all the variables of speed, slope, and distance, Cranford points out that "it is only by putting on greens that one learns to putt on greens" (p. 147). Once again, you learn what you practice.

Of course, the ideal is to practice putting on greens on the course using mastery practice. However, if practice is restricted to the putting green, at least make putting green practice as similar to playing conditions as possible. As discussed previously, remove hole markers from the holes, line up the putts, and keep some kind of score. Above all, don't just run onto the putting green and slap the ball around carelessly. If practice is done carelessly, then carelessness may very well be what is learned; and carelessness will certainly not enhance one's playing ability.

FIGURE 6-3   Player encountering some of the environmental challenges of golf—lakes, trees, bushes, and rain. In addition to the obvious rain suit and umbrella being used to keep the player and his equipment dry, notice the towel hung in the spokes of the umbrella and the player holding his club under the umbrella so as to keep the grip dry.

When Not Playing Regularly, Keep in Touch

There are golf vacations, and there are also vacations from golf. Daily work schedules and family responsibilities can create circumstances where the opportunity to play is restricted, resulting in a loss of confidence, fear of playing, and a feeling of actually having forgotten how to play. Such golfers believe they will be lost when they step onto the first tee, that it will be a struggle to regain their rhythm, that playing is hardly worth the effort. So, instead of heading for the course, they stay home and engage in some safer activity such as watching TV or doing yardwork.

It is simply a reality that there will be times and circumstances when play is restricted. But it is not absolutely necessary to lose touch with the game or lose all confidence during these times of limited play.

South African golf star, Gary Player, described his school days in England when his playing time was curtailed by homework and inclement winter weather. He would simply swing a club a little bit every day in order to retain the feel. It might even have been done indoors, but at least he stayed in touch with the game. Gary's example suggests a hierarchy of ways in which to cope with limited playing time:

The 45-Minute Round

Perhaps you can't hit balls and play 18 holes every day. But maybe you could stop on the way home from work or go out in the evening and play just a few holes for 45 minutes or so. Joggers manage to work in their 45-minute run everyday. Why can't dedicated golfers work in their 45-minute round? Furthermore, if you're a jogger as well as a golfer, combine the two activities for added efficiency in time management.

A Bag of Balls

Stop by the driving range and hit a bag of balls for a half hour every other day. This should, at least, keep you in touch with the mechanics of the swing. Perhaps on alternate days, you could spend the half hour on the putting green.

A Few Minutes in the Backyard

Pick up a club and swing it in the backyard each day. Keep the driver, 5 iron, wedge, and putter in the garage, so that you trip over them on the way into the house. Then before going in and settling down for the evening, swing each club a few times, going through the mental gymnastics of playing a few holes. This should take about five to ten minutes. Don't forget to rehearse a few chips and putts. It is important to stay in touch with these important strokes.

The Mirror Exercise

Stand in front of a full-length mirror and review your swing on a daily basis. This should help in retaining the image of the swing and encourage a regular review of useful swing thoughts. It may help to cut off an old club just below the grip to hold onto during this exercise. In fact, indoor practice aids are available that add some weight to a shortened shaft, creating the sensation of a full-length club.

Swing Thoughts

If a mirror isn't available, at least review your swing thoughts from time to time. Write down a few brief reminders of what was working the last time you played, and then review those notes occasionally. In this way, you will at least be doing a little practice in your head, if not on the course.

The objective of each alternative in this hierarchy is to stay in touch with the game. That is, keep loose, retain a feel for the club and the swing, and, perhaps most importantly, *think the game.* There is no question that golf involves physical mechanics, but it also involves a great deal of thinking. Regular practice of both the physical mechanics and the psychological thinking, in some form or another, is necessary to stay in touch with the game.

If the fearful golfer, who hasn't played for a period of time, employs one of these daily exercises, it is likely that he or she will confidently welcome the next opportunity to play. The swing will be loose, the swing thoughts will be fresh, and the golfer is likely to feel that the hiatus from golf hasn't been nearly as long as it actually has been.

Breaking a Slump

Sometimes golfers find themselves in a slump, seemingly getting nowhere with practice or play. When a slump occurs, consider the following:

Stop Practicing and Playing for a While

You are practicing and learning mistakes at the moment, which can't be very productive or rewarding; and it may totally turn you off to golf.

After a Hiatus, Return to the Fundamentals

It's possible that some very basic things have been inadvertently forgotten. Check your grip, stance, body position, and swing plane. Make sure your head is staying in position. Check notes on what you were doing when previously playing well. Above all, don't start experimenting with a variety of new techniques. This may only confuse the situation and make the slump worse.

Focus on Mechanics Rather Than Outcomes

Once executing the fundamental mechanics of the swing properly again, don't worry if the ball doesn't immediately go perfectly straight or directly into the hole. Persist with the proven fundamentals and look for gradual gains in the results. The only goal at this point should be to execute properly.

If the Slump Continues, Take a Lesson

Your problem may be just a simple adjustment that a pro can spot immediately. But even if some painful changes are required that entail lots of work, at least you'll be confident that you're on the right track, and practice will again be fruitful.

Why Some Golfers Never Seem to Improve

Golf is a lot like life in many respects. It involves risks, obstacles, endless struggles, and, like the game of life, is often unfair.

But in one particular way it strikes me that golf is not like life. Usually in life, when things are done repeatedly, a person tends to get better at them. For example, young children are pretty clumsy at brushing their teeth, at first. But after a bit of repetition or practice, they become so skilled at toothbrushing that it becomes almost automatic. The same relationship between repetition and improved, automatic skill occurs with driving a car, using a typewriter, and using your head in various academic pursuits.

But how many golfers have you known, perhaps to include yourself, who have played golf for years and years and yet seem to never get any better? There's the guy who had the funny swing 15 years ago, and he's still got it today. There's the member who could never get out of the sand, and still can't. There's the 25 handicapper who's been stuck at that handicap for the past 25 years, and he'll never get any better.

I can understand the two handicapper, or even the ten handicapper who has reached the limit of his potential and can hardly improve anymore. After all, golf is a difficult game. But, really! A 25 handicap over years and years of regular play? It would seem that some improvement should occur from this level of play. It's like being of normal intelligence yet being a D student all one's life. With a little concerted effort, anybody should be able to get C's and B's.

Maybe therein lies the answer to this seeming paradox. Even though golfers play regularly, they may not be working as hard, or as systematically, at the game as it may seem. For example, hanging around the putting green and knocking a few putts around before playing may be done year after year. But does this unconscious ritual constitute systematic putting practice leading to improvement?

Regarding swing flaws or difficulties with certain shots, most high-handicap golfers are likely to play with other high-handicap golfers. As they exchange tips and suggestions, they probably end up substituting one swing flaw for another swing flaw. If they never take lessons, not only do they continue practicing their old ways, but they never have the opportunity to identify and practice the correct techniques which might lead to improved play.

Furthermore, does the unimproved golfer really practice or play as much or as regularly as it might seem? Indeed, she may have been a club member for years, and you may even see her around the course a lot in the summer. But how many 18-hole rounds per week are actually completed? And what about layoffs, like for the whole winter? The amount of practice and play that the great players devoted to their games on their way to improvement is legendary.

So, perhaps it is understandable why so many golfers never seem to improve. And maybe, in retrospect, it is not even so unlike life, in general. Consider people who make the same investment mistakes over and over again, or take another job with the same headaches as the one they just quit, or pick a new spouse who is no different than the one who came before.

Perhaps it's part of the human condition to resist learning. Or, at least, learning might be said to be difficult without expert analysis of past mistakes and systematic practice of new directions.

Chapter 7

Playing: The Total Experience

Finally, the bottom line, an actual round of golf—time to stop preparing, stop practicing, stop talking—time to produce. If it's a competitive round of golf, electricity is in the air. Everything you've been working toward is on the line. Fun, challenge, excitement—this is what it's all about.

Playing a round of golf requires a disciplined game plan, a warm-up phase, handling first tee and early hole jitters, staying focused throughout the round, and dealing with various unexpected, difficult situations that can arise during a round. The following explores these various challenges in playing golf.

Game Plan

Even though each round of golf involves a standard 18 holes, there is actually nothing standard about any 18 holes. The holes will differ each round depending on the specific course being played, the layout of the course on that given day (i.e., tee positions, pin placements), the weather conditions, and the current state of your motivation and ability. Taking all these things into account, a strategy must be engineered for dealing with the present circumstances.

Let's say that the course being played is relatively short with narrow fairways, requiring accuracy rather than distance. Under these circumstances, plan to use the driver sparingly, deferring to the 3 wood for many tee shots to ensure a more accurate result. Plan beforehand the specific holes on which to use the 3 wood, as well as the specific holes where the driver could reap rewards. Stick with this plan no matter what happens once the round is under way.

On certain very difficult holes, entertain a strategy of playing safe. That is, allow for a chance at par, but be sure to get a bogey. If it's a par-four hole with a lot of water, plan to tee off with a 2 or 3 iron short of the water, knock another safe iron shot short of the green, then pitch up close providing a putt at par but a sure two-putt bogey five. Again, this should be part of the game plan determined before the round, not something decided in the heat of action (Figure 7-1).

FIGURE 7-1   Challenging hole with trees and water which must be taken into
account when planning strategy for tee shot and approach to green.

In rainy or cold weather conditions, make a plan for keeping dry and warm and yet free to swing. The plan might involve a certain choice of clothing but also a strategy for handling your equipment efficiently so that it stays in playable condition.

If you happen to be stuck with a bit of a slice in your game, you might plan to live with it for the day by aiming a little left on each shot, rather than trying to work it out during an important round.

Other strategy considerations might include the swing thoughts you want to concentrate on during the round. Keep them simple, think about them only during your practice swing, and don't waste any time getting to the ball and executing them before distractions set in. Once over the ball, just get super-relaxed and let your final thought be nothing but keeping your head still and focused on the ball.

Warm-up

Once a game plan is settled on, it's time to take it to the practice area and warm up. The best initial activity may be to hit a few putts, followed by a few easy swings with a short club such as a nine iron. After the muscles are warmed up through this gentle golfing activity, stretching may be useful, with the primary focus on the back and torso, the areas of the body where limberness is essential for a complete golf swing. Although it is beyond the scope of this book to provide a prescribed series of exercises, many other written resources are available for guidance in this regard (e.g., Jobe and Schwab, 1986). If you have specific back problems, consult a physical therapist or other health professional to determine the best exercises for you.

Now you are ready to begin seriously warming up the components of your game. Return to the putting green and plan to spend at least half of the warm-up time on putting. Get used to the speed of the greens; hit a number of long, medium, and short putts; and end up by hitting combinations of these putts using only one ball, similar to what will be required on the course. As suggested earlier, take the little pins out of the holes and putt everything out. Also, practice quietly and seriously. Social chatter will be absent when you are standing over your initial putt on the first green (Figure 7-2).

Having completed your putting warm-up, spend a little time on the chipping green, hitting the little greenside shots that will be required out on the course. Don't forget to hit a few sand shots. Sand shots are also nice cushioned shots for the first full swings of the day.

Moving to the practice tee, take the driver and swing it gently in an increasingly wider arc. Just swing the clubhead back and forth like a pendulum, keeping your head in position while the weight of the clubhead gently tugs at the muscles, tendons, and joints of

FIGURE 7-2 **Player warming up quietly on putting green.**

MENTAL SPOTLIGHT   Getting It There

How to hit it as well on the course as you do on the range

Joe hits the ball great on the driving range, but when he gets on the course, he loses it. A golf swing is a golf swing, right? If you can hit long, straight shots on the range, why can't you do the same on the course?

The problem is focus. It changes from the range to the course. When you practice, you focus on how impact feels or how the ball looks flying off the clubface, often disregarding distance and direction, the two mandatory ingredients for successful play on the course.

You know how it goes:

"How you hitting 'em, Joe?"

"Great—getting 'em up in the air today. Feels good." What Joe hasn't realized is that the ball actually is sailing about 15 yards left of where he's aligned, so he's getting about 10 more yards than usual.

Joe's also relaxed on the range. He doesn't care about the one or two fat shots or the duck hooks sailing into the trees: The bad ones don't count when you practice. But when you get to the first tee, everything counts. Those trees on the left loom large, and suddenly hooks are a real threat. Since Joe hasn't done anything on the range to prepare himself for this reality, his muscles and mind fill with tension.

Joe's neglecting other important parts of the game on the range, too: playing from different lies, creating shots and shotmaking, and addressing the ball with his playing companions watching him. Like Joe, you must prepare yourself for these things when you're on the driving range or stepping to the first tee will be a shock to the system. Here's how to make sure you're ready.

Be Precise and Careful

Pick a target out on the range. Judge its distance just as you do on the course. Take the appropriate club and go through your usual preshot alignment routine for each swing. Carefully and deliberately hit the shot to the target. Keep doing it until you get it right.

If you're practicing with the driver, imagine a corridor defined by land features to serve as your fairway. Trees, flags, humps in the ground, whatever they are—align yourself precisely and hit the ball down the "fairway."

Prepare Under Pressure

It would be great to take a relaxed, carefree driving-range swing to the course. But face it, it just doesn't happen! Rather than fight your feelings around the course, change your practice habits. Put some demands on yourself on the range. For example, if you topped a ball on the course, you wouldn't move cheerfully on to the next shot. Instead, you'd stop, take a practice swing, and give serious thought to what could have gone wrong. Treat bad shots on the range the same way. Practice is no joke, so don't laugh off the bad ones. Expect more from yourself, and when you do hit a bad shot, stop, gather yourself, and prepare fully for the next shot.

Think about on-course situations on the range. You'll be faced with difficult shots out there, so get ready. Hit some knock-down short irons, a few shots out of divots or bad lies, and some deliberate hooks and slices. Find a place to hit from sidehill or downhill lies. Hit a couple from rough. These are situations you'll face during a round, so take your time and prepare completely for each one.

Have you heard the adage "Quitting on a good one?" That's backwards. It should be "Hit a good one when you quit." The last ball in the bucket may be the most important. The pressure is real: Only one ball left and you want it to be a good one. You hate to leave the practice tee with some ugly flight pattern in mind. So bear down, concentrate, and hit the shot you want, just as you have to do out on the course.

Inoculate Yourself to Social Influences

Golfers joke around on the range and socialize with their playing companions, casually swatting a few balls at their leisure. This demeanor violates everything discussed above. It also comes back to haunt you when those jovial buddies suddenly become deadly serious on the course. The jokes stop and everybody's watching. Are you ready?

Don't yuck it up with the guy next to you during practice. Focus on what you are doing in your own quiet little world. Or alternate with a playing companion, hitting precise practice shots while watching each other. This is how it is on the course. If you want to experience social pressure on the range, ask a friend to watch you hit a few drives. Tell him—out loud or to yourself—you're going to show him how it's done (that is, after all, the implication on the course). Remember, a good golf swing on the range doesn't do much for you if you can't perform with it on the course.

your back, neck, and torso. Once you are loose, start with the shortest club (the wedge) and hit some gentle pitch shots, working up to the full swing with the wedge. Then gradually move to longer and longer clubs, hitting a few balls with each, until hitting the final warm-up shots with the driver.

In the ideal situation, end the warm-up by working through the clubs that will be called for on the first few holes of the upcoming round. Hit the required clubs in sequence, visualizing the situations to be faced on the early holes. Put your swing on automatic pilot as much as possible at this point, focusing only minimally on mechanics. Pay particular attention to alignment and distance, which will be of critical importance on the course. Conclude this final stage of the warm-up by hitting a good shot with the club you will be using to begin the round (e.g., the driver on the first tee). This is the image that should be freshest in memory when beginning the round.

The First Tee

For the novice golfer, the first tee may be a harrowing experience. For the expert, it may be a peak moment. In either case, particularly if other people are standing around and observing, an increased degree of motivation will be present for the first *real* shot of the day (Figure 7-3).

Wherever you fall on the continuum from fear to excitement, the solution for dealing with increased motivation is the same—keep it simple. Focus on only one or two things and, interestingly, the heightened motivation may actually enhance your likelihood of suc-

FIGURE 7-3 Foursome on first tee with other golfers observing as they await their turn to play.

MENTAL SPOTLIGHT   Psyche Holes

Keep a steady head during these three vital stretches and
the rest of your round will take care of itself

I know the most important holes on your golf course. No matter who you are, no matter where you're playing. True, every golfer will face a flip wedge over water that makes his knees knock, and every course has its impossible par four. But that's not what I'm talking about. Certain holes present a greater mental challenge than others, simply because of where they occur in the round. If you can negotiate these "psyche" holes, your round is fairly secure.

The first set is holes one, two, and three. The opening holes set the tone for the rest of a round, the way the opening drive is key to a football game. You'll often see a team take the opening kickoff, thunder down the field, and punch in a touchdown before their opponents know what hit them. Their enthusiasm and aggressiveness make an impact and set the tone for the rest of the day.

Take the first trio of holes as a whole. It's nice to par or birdie the first hole, but it's not enough to carry you through the rest of the round. How many times have you followed up a birdie on the first with a double-bogey on the second? Think of it this way: You're not done with the first hole until you putt out on number three. If you par or birdie the first, don't get complacent; if anything, you must bear down even harder on the second and third.

The key to the first three holes is the warm-up. Along with loosening your muscles by hitting a few balls and familiarizing yourself with the speed and conditions of the greens, a smart warm-up includes plotting strategy. While hitting balls, mentally map out a plan for attacking the first three holes— and only the first three. When you step to the tee on each, you'll know exactly what you have to do, which helps focus your concentration.

The second set of psyche holes is 10, 11, and 12. On these three, the challenge is to keep the momentum going from the front nine. In basketball, many games are won or lost in the first five minutes of the second half: One team comes out of the locker room cold, the other team goes on a hot streak, and the cold team never recovers. Ide-

ally, you'd go directly from the ninth green to the 10th tee, but many golfers make a stop at the halfway house. That's not always a good idea. You come off a good front nine, the energy and adrenaline are up, and you toss down some junk food. No surprise then that the first three holes on the backside are a mess.

Making the turn should not be a lunch break. A round of golf is an athletic event and you're in the middle of it. Don't let down. If you need to use the facilities or get a drink, do so quickly and remain focused. Give yourself a halftime pep talk and formulate your plan for the next three holes. Another suggestion: Eat for success. Water is the true drink of champions, and if there's fruit available, grab some for energy. Your meal comes after the round.

The final set of psyche holes is the last three. You've got to be able to "bring it home." Certain relief pitchers are "closers," brought in to shut down the opposition in the last inning or two. In golf, we all have to be closers in every round we play. Many great scores have turned into mediocre ones because the golfer was unable to hold it together down the stretch.

When you reach number 16 tee, pause for a moment and take a breath. This is the two-minute warning, the seventh-inning stretch. What follows separates the men from the boys, the weak of heart from those with intestinal fortitude. Keep your spirits high: This is an opportunity to prove yourself. Go for it.

Seem a bit scary? Your swing keys will carry you through. Let them be your main focus; they are good insurance against disaster. For example, you may be overeager to see a good shot, which leads to coming out of the swing too soon and hitting the killer slice. In this case, set one goal for yourself during each swing: Stay down! Stick with it down the stretch. It's not important what the swing key is; just make sure it's one—and only one—and that you remain committed to it until you finish. Accomplish this, and the results will take care of themselves.

By Thomas N. Dorsel, *GOLF Magazine* (March, 1993). Copyright © 1992, 1993 by *GOLF Magazine*.

cess. In contrast, if you try to think of too many things, your attention will probably be so scattered that you won't succeed in executing anything properly.

The only thoughts that are absolutely necessary at these critical moments are to *relax* and *keep your head down*. Basically, make sure you are looking at the ground when the ball is in flight. Once aware of the ground with no ball there, then look up to see what happened. This isn't a bad idea for all shots, but it is especially crucial when in the pressure cooker.

To facilitate keeping your head down, say to yourself, "If this shot goes awry, I don't want to see it anyway. If it goes well, it will be enough that everyone else saw it." In reality, you'll end up seeing it, too. All you have to give up is seeing the first second or two of the ball's flight (which is not asking too much) in order to enhance your chances of hitting a successful shot.

The Two Nines

The first nine, or front nine in golf vernacular, differs from the second, or back nine, in a number of ways. On the front nine the golfer is still loosening up and getting a feel for the swing. He is trying to get off to a good start and build confidence for the rest of the round. *Patience* is required. There are a lot of holes left, and he needs to hang in there no matter what the outcome of the early holes.

The back nine, in contrast, finds the golfer fully loosened up. He knows the condition of his game. He knows which shots can be confidently attempted and which ones he had better use sparingly. He may be in a position to put the finishing touches on what has started out to be a very good round, or he may find himself in need of making a comeback. The back nine is a venue for *courage*. When the pressure mounts, the golfer will have the opportunity to see what he is made of.

The Complete Round

Although the two nines are important and each has its own characteristics, the bottom line is the complete 18-hole round. The 18-hole score is what goes on the scoreboard, in the handicap machine, in the record books. When people ask someone how he or she played today, it is the 18-hole score they want to know—not the good nine she had, the great hole he lucked out on, or the extraordinary shot she hit out of the sand trap. All those things are nice and keep golfers coming back, but the 18-hole score is the most significant thing.

For this reason, golfers have to find a way to keep going for the entire 18-hole round. They have to be able to concentrate, control their emotions, and remained focused over a demanding four-hour period. The following are two rather contrasting strategies to consider:

Segment the Round

Sometimes it may aid concentration to segment the round into smaller units. Traditionally, the two nines have been the common units of golf, but there is nothing sacred about nine holes. Why not play three six-hole units, or six three-hole units? The individual golfer is the only one who is going to know or care. In the extreme, one could play one-hole or even one-shot units, evaluating performance on each hole or shot in isolation.

Whatever the size of the segment chosen, deal with only one segment at a time. Each segment is an isolated challenge, evaluated and given credit for in its own right. Let go of the burden of trying to concentrate on the entire round at once. Make a fresh start with each new segment, eventually adding them all together for an entire round, something that was never an immediate, conscious concern while in the heat of the action.

Consolidate the Round

The other side of the coin is to look at the round as a complete unit. There are no segments, just a composite 18 holes. Senior PGA Tour pro Tom Wargo takes this type of thinking to the extreme when he says he views the round as one, giant, par-72 hole. This approach involves looking at the round as a whole rather than as a series of units.

Consolidating the round may help keep one's emotions in line. Wargo isn't going to get overly excited about a birdie, or overly depressed about a double bogey early in the round. Either of these phenomena merely contribute equally weighted strokes along the way to the final putt that makes up the complete score on this lengthy par-72 hole.

Similarly, thinking in terms of an 18-hole unit, as opposed to two nines, is less likely to lead to complacency with a good front nine. Work still remains on the way to a successful, complete 18-hole score. Only after the 18-hole unit is finished can the golfer relax and be proud of herself. There are no consolation prizes such as good nines, nice holes, or great shots. The only thing that counts is the 18-hole score.

On the flip side, a poor front nine does not necessitate total depression, either. Things can still be turned around on the back. The game isn't over yet, and a thrilling finish may still be in store.

Debriefing

When the round is over, review what happened. How many times did your ball find the fairway off the tee? How many greens did you reach in regulation (i.e., one shot on par threes, two shots on par fours, and three shots on par fives)? How many putts did you require? What shots and clubs still need work? Where did mental errors occur?

Remember also to consider what was done well. Where is a pat on the back deserved? Be objective about where you need extra practice. Don't blame one aspect of your game when another is actually the culprit (Figure 7-4).

As was discussed in Chapter Four, make a few notes on the swing thoughts that were working today. Stick them in your golf bag for review before your next round. The next time out, these notes may prevent squandering away the early holes trying to remember what you were doing so well the last time you played.

FIGURE 7-4   Player reviewing score card and making notes following round.

MENTAL SPOTLIGHT   Uncharted Territory

You finally have the chance to play "The Course." You know, the exclusive one in the top 100 or the resort you've been dying to visit. You've spent months (and big bucks) planning the round, and you know this might be your only chance to play the course. Wouldn't it be great to come home and tell your golfing buddies that you shot a great round?

But things rarely work out the way you hope they will. You discover that the fairways are narrower than the ones at your home course, the greens are more undulating, even the flagsticks are a different size.

You don't have the comfort of your home course when you play elsewhere. You don't know every nook, cranny and shortcut, and this unfamiliarity often adds extra strokes to your score. Here are a few tips to help guide you through uncharted territory.

Imagine Similar Holes on Your Home Course

Your home course probably is a mix of easy and difficult holes. You relish the easy holes, and you've learned to handle the difficult ones. But playing a tough hole you've never seen before is an unsettling experience. Instead of being comfortable, you could find yourself in a state of shock: "This is impossible!" "I've never seen a hole like this before!" "Nobody can par this hole!"

In reality, this new hole is no harder than the most difficult hole on your home course. Check the yardage—it's probably about the same as your longest hole. Maybe the unfamiliar hole requires hitting a fade to protect against the out-of-bounds on the left, just like good ol' number three back home. Perhaps you have to lay up in front of the water by the green to guard against a big number, exactly like the 15th hole at your home course.

So it's nothing new. Approach this new monster the way you approach the old monsters back home, the ones you have tamed many times before.

continued

MENTAL SPOTLIGHT   *Continued*

Be Objective in Judging Distances

All golf courses, particularly unfamiliar ones, play tricks with visual illusions. If the flagsticks are shorter than the ones at your home course, for example, the greens will appear farther away than they actually are. Greens with plenty of trouble in front only seem closer than they actually are. Obstacles seem in or out of play when they are actually the opposite. Because of these visual distortions, determining precise distances is vital.

This task has been made easier lately. Precise distances are provided on plates, sprinkler heads and in yardage books. Be sure to use these props and not to forget to seek clarification before the round about whether printed yardages are to the middle or front of a green.

If you don't have the benefit of yardage markers, try this psychological technique from Gary Player: Pick a tree or bush down the side of the fairway that you feel confident is about wedge distance away from you. Then pick another object a bit closer to the hole that is about 9-iron distance, then 8-iron, 7-iron and so on. Continue this way until you reach the hole—which may turn out to be a 4-iron shot.

Hit the Club You Are Supposed to Hit, and Hit It the Way You Are Supposed to Hit It

In an unfamiliar situation, decisions often feel like crapshoots. Hit a 6-iron? But it looks like a 7. How are you supposed to know when you've never played the hole before? Such indecision might lead to a tentative swing or a last-minute adjustment that conforms more to gut feeling than to objective judgments.

Once you've checked yardages and conditions (wind, lie, and so on) and made the appropriate club selection, don't hold back. You've picked the right club, now hit it the way it is supposed to be hit.

Be Realistic in Your Expectations

Despite all your objectivity and seriousness, new courses are still going to jump up and grab you occasionally, visual illusions are still going to play tricks on you and the shock value of certain unexpected holes is still going to put extra pressure on your game.

Be realistic. Although taking the proper steps will put you in a good position to play well, don't tee it up with the hope of having a career round. Yes, you want to play your best, but don't allow unrealistic expectations about shooting a great round ruin the fun of new challenges, beautiful scenery and the memories of a once-in-a-lifetime round of golf.

Competition: The Ultimate Challenge in Golf

"If it doesn't matter whether you win or lose, why do they keep score?" said Adolph Rupp, the University of Kentucky's legendary basketball coach. Competition is the ultimate challenge. Success in practice and friendly games is one thing, but it's quite another to be able to produce when the pressure is on and the athlete is on the line.

In the competitive arena, golf holds a special place in sport as a game of honor. Players monitor their own progress, call rule infractions on themselves, and report their scores without the aid of umpires or referees. Most of the time golfers are not even under the scrutiny of spectators.

Having the trust of fellow competitors is a distinct privilege. But it also brings with it the serious responsibility for understanding the various technicalities of the game, such as the handicap system, the basic forms of competition, score keeping, and the rules of play.

The Handicap System

The handicap system is intended to provide a way for golfers to enjoy a fair, competitive game despite varying levels of expertise. The system allows beginners to play experienced players without being totally frustrated, and experienced players to be challenged even though their talents far exceed the developing skills of their novice opponents.

Before getting into detail, there are a few terms to be introduced which are necessary for understanding the handicap system: (1) *Par for the course* is the total of the par values for all the holes that make up the course. (2) The *Course Rating* is a measure of the difficulty of the course. Just because a hole is a par five does not mean that it typically plays to that score. For example, if a tournament were played on the course, the average score on a given par five might actually be 4.6. On the other hand, some holes may play harder than their par values. A very difficult par three might produce an average score of 3.4. All the holes on a course can be rated in this manner, with the course rating being the total of the average scores for all the holes. The course rating is usually within a stroke or two of the actual par for the course. (3) The *Slope Rating* is a relatively new index of course difficulty which can be used to compare courses more accurately than is possible with course ratings alone. It is beyond the scope of this book to describe the slope system in detail, but let it suffice to say that slope ratings usually range between 100 and 140. As an example, a 129 slope rating would indicate a more difficult course than would a 112 slope rating.

With this terminology in mind, this is how the handicap system works: Every time an 18-hole round is played (combining nines from successive outings is permitted, if you rarely have time to play complete 18-hole rounds), the 18-hole score is reported to the pro shop where it is put in a computer. When 20 scores are accumulated (and after each successive score thereafter), the computer program calculates a handicap in the following way: *It takes the best ten of the last 20 scores, calculates the average of those ten scores, and the handicap is the difference between that average and the course rating.* To illustrate, if the average of the best ten scores out of the last 20 scores is 87, and the course rating is 71, then the handicap would be the difference between 87 and 71, which is 16. Now, if a golfer with a 16 handicap plays another golfer with a handicap of ten, the 16 handicapper is allowed to deduct six strokes (the difference between the two handicaps) from her score in order to have a fair game with her ten-handicap opponent.

The slope rating becomes a factor when a golfer goes to another course. (The following is a little complex, so read carefully.) In addition to the handicap, the computer will provide each golfer with a *handicap index* based on the slope rating for the course where the handicap has been established. If the golfer's handicap is 12, the handicap index might be 12.8 or 11.3. The handicap index is not exactly the same as the handicap because it takes into account the level of difficulty of the course as reflected in the course's slope rating.

When a golfer goes to another course, instead of taking his handicap, he takes his handicap index. Since the new course will have its own level of difficulty and its own slope rating, the handicap index can be used to tell the golfer what a fair handicap should be for the new course. This is done for the golfer by comparing his handicap index to a chart available at every course. The professionals at the new course will be happy to help with this procedure if they are given the handicap index.

Abuse of the Handicap System

The handicap system has considerable potential for dishonesty. Everyone knows golfers with artificially low handicaps that can never be lived up to; and everyone knows golfers with inflated handicaps that make them instant winners in handicap events. It's like an open secret—something that everyone knows about but nobody openly discusses.

There are obvious ways to blatantly manipulate one's handicap. If a low handicap is desired, turn in only low scores. Similarly, a high handicap comes from turning in only high scores.

Being slightly less blatant, one's handicap can be artificially lowered by accepting putts as *gimmes*. A gimme (contraction for "give me," as in "give me the putt") is a widespread custom among social golfers where a player is charged with a stroke for a short putt but is excused from actually executing the putt. The practice of giving and accepting gimmes is a violation of the rules of golf when a player's objective is to record an 18-hole score. Gimmes may be responsible for lowering scores by two or three stokes per round, and handicaps by a similar amount.

But there are much more subtle ways in which a well-intentioned player might manipulate the handicap system, particularly to create an artificially lower handicap.

For example, handicaps are calculated every month. As described above, they are based on the best ten out of the last 20 scores. Handicap lists also indicate how current the handicap is by listing the month that the last score was posted. Naturally, the more current the handicap, the more valid it is, as it reflects how the golfer is playing at the present time. If 20 scores have been entered over the last two or three months, the handicap might be considered to be truly current.

But some very low-handicap golfers have only one or two scores per month, stretching their 20 scores out over a 10- to 15-month period. Can a score submitted a year ago be a valid reflection of how one is playing at the present time? Furthermore, how could a scratch-handicap (zero-handicap) golfer maintain such a low handicap by playing only once or twice per month?

One way a golfer could "honestly" achieve this low handicap on a few scores is by doing the following, which is a second way of subtly manipulating the handicap system. Every time he plays a bad front nine, he quits and doesn't play the back nine so a high score doesn't have to be turned in. Or if the back nine is already started and the score begins to get out of hand, he manufactures an excuse to quit, starts messing around, or turns the round into a practice session. Any of these maneuvers will provide a "legitimate" excuse for not turning in the higher than desirable score.

Such subtle manipulation of the handicap system can happen quite innocently. When a golfer is playing poorly, he often gets tired a bit faster and may lose interest in the game for the moment. It's quite easy to succumb to the temptation to quit, go home, and come back later for another try. It may not even occur to the golfer that he has avoided posting a score that would be less than flattering to his low handicap.

Yet another way in which a golfer might unwittingly keep a handicap unreasonably low is by coming back the next day to finish a good round that was ended prematurely the day before because of rain or darkness. This is permissible according to the handicap system, and the procedure is reasonable if done consistently. The problem that arises, however, is that it is not done consistently. Rarely do golfers go out of their way to come back the next day to finish rounds in which they were playing poorly. Again, the result is an artificial lowering of the handicap.

The handicap system is a wonderful idea. It is a way to make all golfers comparable when it comes to competitive events in which such comparability is desirable. But it will only work when handicaps are valid.

Why would golfers want an artificially low handicap? The only plausible answers are that (1) they want to appear to be better golfers than they actually are, or (2) they want to gain entry into prestigious tournaments that require handicaps within a certain low range.

What a shame. Golf is a difficult game. Very low, valid handicaps are hard to come by, and few players should expect this of themselves. The United States Golf Association (*GOLFWEEK*, 1993) listed statistics a few years ago indicating that the average male handicap nationally was 16, the average female handicap 29. Only about 6 percent of the males and .4 percent of the females had handicaps of five or lower. At the other extreme, 12 percent of the males had handicaps over 25, and over a fourth of the females had handicaps over 35.

To artificially lower one's handicap only puts added pressure on the golfer, making it difficult for him or her to win in events involving handicaps or to compete productively in tournaments that are reserved for only the best players. Of course, an inflated handicap gives a golfer an unfair advantage in handicapped tournaments, which all the more destroys the virtue of handicapped competition.

Two solutions come to mind. The first is reminiscent of the verifiability issue in nuclear arms negotiations. Verifiability of handicaps could be achieved by posting for handicap calculation only those scores that occur in official, well-monitored tournaments. Unfortunately, such a system would eliminate many players from the handicap system because many golfers never play in formal competition.

The better solution might be to appeal to the dignity of the game itself. As stated earlier, golf is the only game that is largely self-monitored. Golfers keep their own score, call rule violations on themselves, and don't employ referees and umpires as other sports do. Golfers should also be able to monitor their own honest handicap. Such self-regulation only enhances the dignity of the game of golf and increases its competitive enjoyment for everyone.

Jockeying for Position on the First Tee

It is not uncommon for golfers to join up with other golfers whom they only know in passing, or whom they have just met. Most golfers have experienced this when invited to play as a guest or when they unexpectedly pick up a game at their home course with someone they have never played with before.

It is also not uncommon for the following conversation to occur as the round is planned with the new golfing companion:

"Why don't we see if we can get up a little game (wager, that is)?" Don Driver asks. Receiving a tentative, but affirmative, nod from Wally Wedge, his new acquaintance, Don pops the big question, "WHAT IS YOUR HANDICAP?"

Wally clears his throat, avoids eye contact, and begins to work the tee box like a used car salesman. "Well," he says, "officially my handicap is nine—at least that's what it says in the pro shop—but I've been trying to break in a new set of clubs and I'm actually playing to around a 13. Now, if I were playing with my old clubs, I'd probably be around 11 or 12, but there is no way that I'd ever be a nine."

Don replies, "Yeah, I know what you mean. My handicap is 14, but I've had a bad back and been busy at work, so I'm playing so bad I haven't broken 90 in two months. If I were healthy and playing regularly, I still should only be around a 17. But right now, realistically, my handicap has to be 20."

Wally, feeling a sense of kinship in that he is playing with another used car salesman, suggests that he give Don three strokes on the front nine, and that they adjust on the back. And so on and so on. . . .

The above conversation reflects something short of abuse of the handicap system, but it is still a far cry from how the handicap system was designed to work. A golfer's posted

MENTAL SPOTLIGHT   The Case for Serious Golf

Whatever happened to the serious golfer—the one who used to tee the ball up and not touch it again until it was in the hole? The one who actually used to putt the ball into the cup 18 times every round? The one who played a simple game of golf, where winning was based on who shot the lowest score for 18 holes, not on who had the most greenies, sandies, chippies, poleys or bingo-bango-bongos?

Back in the late '50s and early '60s, people played a serious game of golf. I don't necessarily mean expert golf, just serious. Many people shot in the 80s or 90s, but they played serious golf.

By that I mean a pure and simple game played by a standard set of rules. They completed all the holes, counted all their shots, recorded all their scores and generated accurate and reasonable handicaps. When I was a junior golfer in the '50s and '60s I played serious golf, and I assumed that as I grew older I would continue to be able to play serious golf. But here it is two decades later, and I look around and there's nobody to play with.

I realize I'm overstating it. I occasionally run into other serious golfers, and I jump at the chance to play with them. But in general, golfers nowadays are making a mockery of the game.

For example, many golfers today are afraid to keep their score. "Let's play match play." "Give me an 'X' on that hole." "I'll just drop a ball here instead of going back to the tee." "Anything inside the length of the flagpole is a gimme." Why do you think scores soar in the club championship? Because finally you're seeing something that resembles an accurate score.

This, of course, assumes that you can get someone to play in the club championship. Many golfers won't play competitively unless they can disguise their scores in a best-ball event or a captain's-choice scramble, where some ridiculously low team score goes on the board and saves the golfer from revealing how he really played.

Golf, in the more serious sense, was meant to be a game where the individual puts himself on the line and stands or falls based on his own talent or lack thereof. So why are there so few serious golfers left in the world? It may be because expectations have become unrealistic. People think they should play better than they do, and they're embarrassed when they shoot what should really be considered a very respectable score.

And why do they think they should play better than they do? Probably because their main frame of reference is what they see on television—the best golfers in the world, all warmed up, playing the final holes of a round, at a time when, as they've already proved by making the cut, they're on their game. This level of play isn't representative of even the typical touring professional.

If only we could see some of the stars when they are missing cuts, struggling on the early holes of a round, blowing three-foot putts—then, maybe, modern golfers would develop more realistic expectations for their own play.

Beyond this, the amateur golfer needs more opportunities to compete seriously. Having one's score posted would then be less of a shock, and seeing what everyone else was really shooting would provide a realistic frame of reference.

Opportunities to compete might include old-fashioned president's and governor's cup tournaments, along with the traditional club championship. The latter event, in fact, might be elevated to a position of special honor, as it used to be. I sometimes fantasize that every golfer at a golf club should be required, as a stipulation of his membership, to play in the club championship. The true champion would then be given the recognition that such an accomplishment deserves.

Clubs could also hold less formal monthly tournaments—just for the sake of competing, rather than for costly prizes. Or a challenge ladder might be set up, giving golfers a way to seek out whatever level of competition they want.

There are, of course, those who will say, "Hey, I just want to have fun, socialize, drink a few beers. What's all this seriousness stuff about? Are you trying to take all the fun out of golf?"

I refer this person to a statement by the late Adolph Rupp, the famed basketball coach at the University of Kentucky, who was frequently criticized for being too hard on his players. His rejoinder was: "My boys get their fun out of winning national championships."

And I get my fun out of playing serious golf. If I want to have a social gathering with food and drink, I have a party. If I want to get some exercise, test my developing skills, compete and win, I play golf. Naturally I accept other folks' desires to have a social event—to ride around in golf carts, drink beer and call it an afternoon of golf. That's fun for

continued

handicap *is* his handicap. If he is playing regularly, like a dedicated golfer should, and if he is posting all his scores, then his handicap should be accurate. If two golfers with accurate handicaps are playing, then there should be no need for extended discussion about the game plan on the first tee and no need for adjustment after nine. Indeed, this is the reason the handicap system was designed: to allow players of differing ability, who may not even know each other, to appeal to a universally accepted standard which allows them to compete fairly and compare their scores on an equitable basis.

Therefore, whenever confronted on the first tee with someone who is trying to maneuver around his or her posted handicap, consider the following reply, "My handicap is ten. It is based on scores over the past two months ranging from 76 to 88. Therefore, my score today can be expected to fall somewhere in that range. My handicap is accurate and honest, and assuming you have a similar handicap, we can have a fair game."

The Basic Forms of Competition

The two basic competitive formats are medal play and match play. *Medal play* involves counting all strokes from the first drive to the last putt, and whichever player has the least overall stokes at the end of 18 holes is the winner.

In medal play the only thing that counts is the total 18-hole score; *match play,* in contrast, focuses on one hole at a time. The players compare scores on each hole, and the lowest score wins the hole. It doesn't matter how much lower one or the other golfer's score is on a given hole. All that can be won is the hole, which is one out of 18 holes that can possibly be won. The winner is determined by who wins the most holes.

Although the physical demands are basically the same between the two formats, the psychological challenges can be quite different. Medal play usually involves competing against a whole field of golfers while actually playing with only a few. These circumstances require *playing the course*, that is, shooting for par, virtually ignoring the performance of immediate playing companions. When touring pro John Daly, in a recent U.S. Open, hit two monumental shots to a previously unreachable par five, his playing companion, Payne Stewart, said he didn't even know the feat had occurred. Stewart was completely focused on his own game. He was playing the course, not his opponent.

In medal play golfers do ultimately have to beat those with whom they are playing, but they also have to beat everyone else on the course. Therefore, the best reference point is par for the course, because everyone is shooting for that number. Golfers find that by making the course the chief opponent, beating everyone else will take care of itself.

Consistent with the above, medal play requires steady play, avoiding big scores on holes. Every stroke counts in the final score, which puts a premium on consistency and the ability to endure over the long haul.

Match play, in contrast, is a hole-by-hole affair. It's a battle of wits, head-to-head competition between two individuals who can beat each other not only physically but also psychologically. Match play involves gamesmanship, that constellation of subtle maneuvers intended to unnerve one's opponent, giving the gamesman the upper hand in the match. The story goes, for example, that Ben Hogan would intentionally hit his drives shorter than his opponent so that he could precede his opponent in hitting a good shot to the green, thereby increasing the pressure on the other player.

Match play requires an interesting combination of patience and courage. Patience is epitomized in Bobby Jones' exhortation that all golfers will crack if one keeps throwing pars at them. On the other hand, it is sometimes beneficial to have the courage to go for a risky shot. If the shot is successful, a knockout blow may be delivered to the ambitions of one's opponent. A measure of intestinal fortitude is needed when a comeback is required after getting down a few holes in a match.

Ironically, the best psychological approach to match play may be that which is recommended for medal play: Play the course rather than the opponent. If focus is patiently kept on the par for the course without distraction by the opponent's style of play, victory is likely to be within reach by the end of 18 holes of play. At the same time, don't totally ignore the opponent. If the poor fellow has just hit one out of bounds, for example, it would be foolish to take any chances when a safe bogey will likely win the hole.

Many variations of both medal and match play have been devised over the years to include matches with a partner, team golf, and dozens of other competitive games on which wagers are often based.

Score Keeping

The typical scorecard is arranged in columns, several of which provide information about the layout of the course, whereas others provide space for players to record their scores.

At the very top of the scorecard presented in Figure 8-1, there are spaces for names of the players and each player's handicap. The first column lists the hole numbers, one through 18, with "Out" indicating the end of the first nine holes, and "In" indicating the end of the second nine holes. The terms "Out" and "In" emanate from the design of early courses where the first nine holes went straight out from the clubhouse, and the second nine came straight back in. At St. Andrews in Scotland, generally considered the birthplace of golf, the two nines even shared the same greens going out and in. "Total" on the scorecard indicates the end of the 18 holes.

The second, third, and fourth columns provide information on the yardages for the various holes from the different tees (green, blue, and white). Notice that the totals for each

MENTAL SPOTLIGHT   Variety Is the Spice of Golf—and It Helps Generalize Skills

You have probably known someone who is an excellent golfer—as long as he is playing his home course, at his usual afternoon time, with his same three playing companions.

But put him on a strange course, get him out there in the morning dew, or pair him in another foursome, and it's a different story. This skilled golfer's game seems to fall apart when he is not in his usual circumstances.

From a psychological standpoint, this is called generalization decrement. The golfer has difficulty generalizing, or transferring, his skills from one situation to another. The greater the change from his usual circumstances, the greater the deterioration of his performance.

The remedy for this generalization decrement is quite simple: Practice and play under as many different circumstances as possible. As I have said many times before in various contexts, you learn what you practice. If you practice and play under varied circumstances, you will learn to perform under varied circumstances.

While the remedy is simple, it may not be as easy to implement as it would seem. If you are paying an arm and a leg for dues at a country club, you most certainly are going to play there most of the time. The only thing you can do is take advantage of whatever opportunities you have to play other places, such as on vacations, member-guest tournaments at other clubs, etc. Varying the time of the day may even pose some inconvenience, due to work schedules and family responsibilities, but this variable should be much more under your control. Your playing partners can also become quite fixed, but here's an idea for mixing things up a bit in this regard:

About 20 years ago, my father, Norbert Dorsel, devised a system for efficiently dividing up eight regular playing companions into different weekly foursomes. The system was varied and balanced with regard to who a given golfer's partner was and who his opponents were over a seven-week cycle. If you play bridge, you will recognize it as similar to a party bridge tally. The schedule was laid out as follows:

Dates	Foursome 1	Foursome 2
4/8, 5/27, 7/15	3–7 4–8	1–5 2–6
4/15, 6/3, 7/22	1–6 3–8	2–5 4–7
4/22, 6/10, 7/29	3–6 4–5	1–8 2–7
4/29, 6/17, 8/5	1–4 5–8	2–3 6–7
5/6, 6/24, 8/12	1–7 4–6	2–8 3–5
5/13, 7/1, 8/19	1–2 3–4	5–6 7–8
5/20, 7/8, 8/26	2–4 6–8	1–3 5–7

Note: Players: 1. Ralph; 2. Norb; 3. Henry; 4. Stan; 5. Todd; 6. John; 7. Frank; 8. Gil. Players joined by a dash are partners.

An example of how the schedule is used would be the following: On date 4/08, No. 3 (Henry) would play with No. 7 (Frank) as his partner, and their opponents would be the team of No. 4 (Stan) and No. 8 (Gil). The second foursome would consist of No. 1 (Ralph) and No. 5 (Todd) as partners, with their opponents being the team of No. 2 (Norb) and No. 6 (John).

This system provides for an efficient way to vary your playing companions and thereby enhance your versatility as a competitor. In addition, it will likely make your regular weekly game more fun and interesting.

Thanks, Dad, for this innovative golfing idea. It just adds one more item to the long list of things for which I owe you.

Hole	Green	Blue	White	Hdcp		Handicap		Par			Red	Hdcp
1	404	393	382	3				4			355	1
2	186	172	162	11				3			151	13
3	419	402	389	1				4			328	11
4	142	133	125	17				3			115	17
5	504	468	451	9				5			406	3
6	407	391	375	5				4			352	5
7	165	148	137	13				3			125	15
8	462	446	428	15				5			396	9
9	395	383	372	7				4			337	7
Out	3084	2936	2821					35			2565	
10	331	319	310	18				4			298	14
11	415	400	387	4				4			367	4
12	193	173	151	16				3			137	16
13	382	359	323	10				4			297	12
14	513	495	476	8				5			422	6
15	399	388	370	2				4			348	2
16	186	165	144	14				3			120	18
17	416	403	390	6				4/5			372	10
18	510	490	474	12				5			427	8
In	3345	3192	3025					36			2788	
Tot	6429	6128	5846					71			5353	
Rating	70.9	69.5	68.3					Hdcp			72.3	
Slope	122	119	116					Net			128	

DATE_____ SCORER_____

ATTEST_____

FIGURE 8-1   Typical score card.

Reprinted with permission of Florence Country Club, Florence, SC.

of these columns reflect the different overall yardages for the course, depending on the set of tees from which the golfer chooses to play. The green, blue, and white tees are typically played by male golfers. At the far right on the card are found the red tees, which are usually played by female golfers and allow for considerably shorter yardage on each hole and, in turn, for the whole course.

The "Par" column in the middle of the card lists the par value for each hole, as well as the total par for the respective nines and the complete 18. One idiosyncrasy on the card displayed here should be noted: The par for hole 17 is four from the men's tees, five from the ladies' tees. The length of the hole from the respective tees makes it too easy as a par five for men but too hard as a par four for women. Therefore, different pars are assigned to the hole for the two sexes.

Although par is the expected score for any given hole, some holes are harder to make par on than others. As mentioned earlier in the discussion on course ratings, all par fours are not equally difficult, and some long par threes may actually be harder to achieve par on than some short par fives. The relative difficulty of the various holes is indicated by the numbers in the columns labeled "Hdcp" (handicap). The handicap column on the left side of the card goes with the three sets of men's tees that are adjacent to it; the handicap column on the right side of the card goes only with the ladies' tees.

The way this column works is as follows: When handicap strokes are given in match play, they are given based on the order of difficulty of the holes. That is, the hole marked "1" in the handicap column will get the first stoke, "2" the second stroke, and so on until all the player's strokes are awarded. For example, if four strokes are to be awarded one of the players, the strokes will be given on holes #3, #15, #1, and #11.

The odd-numbered handicap holes are all on the first nine, whereas the even-numbered handicap holes are all on the second nine. This serves to balance the awarding of strokes over holes on the two nines for match play. When playing medal play, where the total score is all that counts, it is irrelevant which holes are awarded strokes, as the total handicap is simply subtracted from the total score at the end of the 18 holes.

Toward the bottom of the score card are found the course ratings and slope ratings for the various sets of tees, as well as spaces to subtract handicaps from total scores to determine net scores (the score after one's handicap has been applied). The rest of the spaces are for recording players' scores, hole by hole, to include nine-hole and 18-hole totals. A couple of spare columns are provided to tabulate any other running scores one might want to keep, such as how many holes a player is ahead in match play.

At the very bottom of the card is a place for the date of the competition, the signature of the one who kept the scores (scorer), and the signatures of all the players whose scores were kept (attest).

Some scorecards are more elaborate, with diagrams of the holes highlighting special features, such as lakes, sand, streams, etc. Yardages from various landmarks to the greens may also be provided on the scorecard or in a separate yardage book offered by some courses.

Rules of Competition

Golf is replete with rules, and understanding them all is a lifetime challenge. Even tour professionals appeal to the rule book to determine the proper procedure for many unanticipated situations that arise on the golf course. Only a thorough reading of the official *Rules of Golf* (United States Golf Association and Royal and Ancient Golf Club of St. Andrews, 1995) will make a golfer truly well versed in this dimension of the game. Tom Watson (1988) has also written a simplified interpretation of the rules, which readers may find to be more user friendly than the official book offered by the United States Golf Association and the Royal and Ancient Golf Club of St. Andrews.

Herein will be described only a general overview of a few of the common rules that will be helpful to know in the early stages of playing golf:

Order of Play

On the first hole, the order of teeing off is usually determined by a flip of the coin, or some other random process. On subsequent tees, the order of play is determined by the order of scores on the immediately preceding hole, with the golfer with the lowest score playing first and the golfer with the highest score playing last. In the case of a tie between two or more players on the immediately preceding hole, the order of play is determined by reviewing back through the preceding holes until the tie is broken.

Other than on the tee, the player who is farthest from the hole is said to be "away" and, therefore, entitled to play first. Sometimes a player who is closer to the hole may hit first (with the permission of the other players), particularly when doing so would speed up play, or when a player off the green is closer to the hole than a player on the green.

Play the Ball as It Lies

Once the ball is placed on a tee and driven down the fairway, it will come to lie on the ground somewhere between the tee and the green. You hope the ball's resting place is in the short grass of the fairway, sitting up as if it were on the bristles of a brush. But it may also be found in the rough, leaning against a root, or resting in a divot hole made by a previous player's shot. In any of these cases, the ball is to be played as it lies. That is, the ball cannot be touched or its position improved by any means. Risk of injury is no excuse for moving the ball. In cases where the ball is against a tree trunk or on a root, a restricted swing, or even a chip shot, might be taken to get the ball safely back into play. Under these circumstances, a player may also invoke the *unplayable lie* rule described later in this chapter.

Playing the ball as it lies is referred to as summer rules. Winter rules are often invoked when the fairway conditions start to deteriorate because of the change of seasons. Winter rules allow the golfer to improve his or her lie in the fairway of the hole that is being played but nowhere else on the course (such as in the rough or in an adjacent fairway). Some courses that are not well manicured call for winter rules all year long.

In general, a golfer plays the ball as it lies whenever possible. Not only is it the way golf was meant to be played, but it will prepare the player for competitive situations where there is no other choice but to play the ball as it lies.

Hazards

Bodies of water (which usually includes their banks) and sand bunkers are examples of hazards. The boundary of a water hazard is marked with yellow stakes or lines.

If a player's ball is seen to go into a water hazard (whether or not the ball can be subsequently found), the rules allow for another ball to be dropped *behind* the hazard as far back as the player chooses, keeping the point of the ball's entry into the hazard between the player and the hole. The simplest way to count the strokes is to count one stroke for the shot into the hazard and one more stroke for the dropped ball. If a water hazard is along the side of a fairway where it is not practical to drop a ball behind the hazard, the hazard is marked by red stakes or lines and is termed a lateral water hazard. In this case strokes are counted the same as before, but a ball is dropped *beside* the spot where the original ball entered the hazard, instead of behind the hazard. The ball should be dropped within two clublengths of the hazard, measuring with the longest club in the bag and marked by the player with two wooden tees. The ball is held shoulder high at arm's length and dropped with no effort to influence the resulting lie of the ball.

In the cases of either of the hazard situations described above, the player has an additional option of returning to the site of the original shot that was hit into the hazard, and replaying the shot. The player's stroke count would include the original shot plus a penalty stroke. That is, if the player's first shot went into the hazard and she elected to return to the tee box, the player would now be hitting her third shot from the tee box.

A bunker is a prepared hollow in the ground where the grass has been removed and replaced with sand. The banks around the sand, in contrast to those around water, are not considered to be part of the hazard. Furthermore, sandy spots found naturally occurring at other areas on the course are not considered to be hazards.

When hitting the ball out of a hazard, the golfer may not touch the hazard with the clubhead prior to the forward swing at the ball. Using golf terminology, the clubhead may not be "grounded." Instead, the club must be held in such a way that the clubhead hovers behind the ball an inch or two above the sand, water, or ground. This rule comes into play mostly in bunkers but also applies if one elects to hit out of a shallow water hazard or even from the bank of a water hazard that lies within the yellow or red stakes demarcating the hazard (Figure 8-2).

FIGURE 8-2   Golfer preparing to hit sand shot. Notice how the clubhead is held so that it hovers over the sand rather than touching the sand.

Ball Lost or Out of Bounds

The boundaries of the course, as marked by fences, walls, roads, or white stakes, are considered to be out of bounds. If a ball crosses any of these boundary lines, another ball must be replayed from the point of the original shot with a penalty of stroke and distance. Said another way, one stroke is counted for the shot hit out of bounds, and another stroke to drop or tee up (in the case of a drive) another ball in the original hitting area. Still more simply stated, the shot is replayed with two strokes added to the score.

If there is uncertainty as to whether or not a ball is out of bounds, the golfer may announce that she is hitting a provisional ball to be played only if the first ball is, indeed, discovered to be out of bounds. Although the penalty strokes described above would still apply if the original ball is found to be out of bounds, the provisional ball saves time by removing the necessity of having to return to the place of the original shot to hit another ball.

The same rules as above also apply to lost balls. That is, the same manner of counting strokes applies, and a provisional ball may be played for balls suspected to be lost in anything other than a water hazard.

Unplayable Lies

If a ball is found in an unplayable situation (i.e., in the middle of a bush, wedged between two boulders, etc.), then the golfer has three choices: (1) Staying within a radius of two clublengths from where the ball lies, he may drop the ball no closer to the hole. (2) Keeping the spot where the ball lies between him and the hole, he may drop the ball as far back as he chooses behind the site of the unplayable lie. (3) He may return to the spot from where the original shot was hit that resulted in the unplayable lie and play another ball. With each of the above alternatives, the player must count the original shot that resulted in the unplayable lie and add a penalty shot for relocating the ball before hitting the next shot.

Ground under Repair and Casual Water

Sometimes areas of a course are unplayable because of unfinished excavation, maintenance, or other conditions, such as the aftermath of a storm. Under tournament conditions these areas will be marked with lines and/or a sign. A similar condition is presented by casual water, which is standing water other than that found in an established water hazard; e.g., a puddle after heavy rains, a lake that has overflowed its banks.

In each of the above cases, the golfer determines the nearest spot playable on the course and which is no closer to the hole than the original position of the ball. The player drops the ball within one club length of that new position, again no nearer the hole. No penalty strokes are applied.

Allowances on the Green

Once the ball is on the putting surface (it should be noted that the fringe of the green is not considered part of the putting surface), the ball may be marked with a small coin or similar object, picked up, cleaned, and replaced when it is the golfer's turn to putt. The ball should also be marked and picked up if it is very near the hole or might otherwise interfere with another player's putt or chip.

The flagstick may be left in the hole during a shot, if the ball is not on the putting surface. If the ball is on the putting surface, the flagstick must either be removed, or another player must hold the flagstick and remove it while the ball is rolling to the hole. The latter condition arises when it is difficult to see the hole because of putting from a great distance or from one level of the green to another.

Old or new ball marks made by balls landing on the green may be repaired. Loose impediments (i.e., stones, sand, twigs, leaves, pine needles), which may be in the line of the putt, may also be removed. It is not permissible to tap down spike marks, little tufts of grass that have been pulled up by golfers walking on the green. It is, however, a courtesy to tap down one's own spike marks when they inadvertently occur, or any other spike marks found after finishing putting.

Chapter 9

Stress and Pressure

"Pressure to me is the fun of the game. . . . There's nobody immune to it. . . . It is what I happen to enjoy. . . . We all practice to get ourselves into this position." These are the words of golfing great Jack Nicklaus reflecting on the pressure of his run at an unprecedented seventh Masters title in April of 1990.

Pressure affects people in different ways. Nicklaus obviously thrives on pressure. Lesser players crumble. Pressure has well-known destructive potential, but it can also have a strengthening impact. An example of the strengthening effect of pressure is the Roman arch where the stones press all the more firmly together under the pressure of the heavy superstructure.

The key to strength under pressure is to channel the anxious energy that results from pressure into concentration on productive swing thoughts. Here are some examples:

Holes 13 and 15 on the course I play lend themselves to unhealthy images of hooking the ball (i.e., a shot which curves sharply from right to left) into water or woods. In order to avoid this dreaded outcome, I know I must relax, keep my head down, and get my weight decisively over to my left side. Of course, these are things I should do on every shot. But thanks to the pressurized situation, I am particularly reminded of it. This means I will use the pressure to my advantage to encourage concentration all the more on the proper technique. Interestingly, sometimes I hit my best drives on these two holes.

Another situation that causes me great concern is a short putt in a critical situation. Here the pressure energizes one of my most adaptive putting thoughts, one that I often forget in less pressurized situations: "I can't force this putt to go in. All I can do is stay down and stroke it smoothly along the line I decide. Having done this, I've done everything within my control regarding the putt." Following this line of thought, I simply do my job and observe the outcome with unemotional acceptance.

Hitting a shot in the presence of spectators can be great fun but also a considerable source of pressure. Once again, I resort to intense concentration on the fundamentals of "relaxing and staying down." I say to myself, "Relax and stay down. If I look up, nobody will see a good shot, including me."

One other situation that presents pressure and requires extra concentration is an unusual lie. For example, the ball may be under tree branches where a missed shot could spell disaster, but a sound swing could save the day. Once again I focus all the more on keeping my head down. I think, "If there is going to be a disaster, I don't want to see it anyway. So stay down and see that contact between the clubface and the ball." There is a little added incentive in this situation. If I look up with all the intrusive branches hanging all around, I am liable to get poked in the eye.

A common thread throughout all of these examples is the age-old fundamental of keeping the head down. Curiously, in some circles the admittedly oversimplified mandate to keep the head down has become an unpopular concept. This seeming conflict is, however, just a matter of semantics. Those who espouse not worrying about keeping the head down are simply suggesting that the chin should not be pressed against the chest, or that a rigid head position should not overly restrict the flow of the swing. These qualifications are, indeed, valid. Still, "keeping the head down" always has been and always will be a useful bit of terminology for the average golfer.

Keeping the head down remains an especially useful concept under pressure, where everyone seems to want to look up. But why does one want to see a disaster? Wouldn't it be better not to see the disaster, even if it does occur? Even more to the point, wouldn't it be better to keep one's head down, and after a momentary delay, see a good shot?

So under pressure there is a great advantage in focusing on the fundamental of keeping the head down. Either a good shot will be struck, or, at least, the disaster won't be seen.

Pressure Can Help or Hurt

In general, pressure will tend to work in the golfer's favor when it is applied to strengths, and will tend to work against the golfer when it occurs in the midst of weaknesses.

Pressure is really just another word for fear; that is, the fear of failure. Fear has long been recognized as a source of motivation, something which energizes all of a person's ongoing activity. Whatever is being done at the moment, whether the behavior is correct or incorrect, is likely to be exaggerated by fear. If a person tends to walk slowly, she will probably walk even more slowly when afraid. If a person tends to swing fast, he will probably swing faster when in a state of fear. If a person's game is sound, it will probably be even sounder, and conversely, if weak, then weaker. Whatever skills, non-skills, or combination thereof is possessed, those behaviors are likely to be exaggerated under pressure.

So, the question is not so much whether pressure, in general, is good or bad. It is more a question of whether pressure is good or bad at the moment. And the answer is quite straightforward: Pressure will help when the golfer is playing well and hurt when the golfer is playing poorly. But what is meant by playing well versus playing poorly?

Skilled performance, or playing well, is more likely to happen for the golfer who (1) is a veteran; (2) is practicing and playing regularly; (3) has a simple swing (less can go wrong); (4) is playing standard shots that have been practiced repeatedly; (5) is on the latter holes of a round after having loosened up; and, (6) is otherwise playing well. It is under these circumstances, when the golfer is already hitting good shots, that a little pressure is likely to exaggerate her skill and contribute to hitting even better shots.

Non-skilled performance, or playing poorly, is more likely to happen for the golfer who (1) is a beginner; (2) is starting up again after a layoff; (3) has a complex swing (more can go wrong); (4) is experimenting or playing risky shots that have not been adequately practiced; (5) is on the earlier holes of a round and not yet loosened up; and, (6) is in a slump. These are the times when mistakes are rampant, and pressure is likely to exaggerate the golfer's errors and result in even worse shots. So a player in this situation should avoid pressure situations until his game comes around.

Based on the above, if you want to give yourself the best chance of withstanding pressure, start well in advance of the anticipated pressure situation to get your game on track. Practice and play regularly, simplifying your swing technique as much as possible. Work on standard shots, as opposed to adding fancy new wrinkles or experimental shots that may break down under pressure. In the heat of competition, avoid taking risks early in the match. A little conservative play may save costly mistakes before you are sufficiently warmed up. Keep expectations realistic and allow for the possibility of a few pressure-induced errors in the weaker areas of your game. When inevitable errors do occur, take them in stride and go ahead and beat your opponent despite a few mistakes.

Jinx Holes and Gambling Shots

Jinx holes (i.e., certain golf holes which are consistently associated with poor play) and gambling shots (i.e., dangerous, experimental shots that have a low percentage of success) are classic examples of where pressure is likely to contribute to failure. By definition, jinx holes are ones which have been regularly associated with failure already. After repeated failures, fear and tension will naturally occur each time the golfer faces the dreaded hole. The fear and tension, in turn, make failure even more likely to occur, leading to a feeling of being "jinxed" on the given hole. The same rationale could also be applied to "jinx shots" or "jinx courses."

The way to overcome jinx holes, shots, or courses is the same way any situation involving fear of failure is overcome; that is, pair the hole, shot, or course with success. The best way to accomplish this success pairing is to practice that very jinx hole until it is done correctly. This means actually going out to the particular hole and taking the "jinxed" shots over and over again until you see yourself do it correctly and have an image of success in the given situation. Favorable images of success, and some newly practiced correct behaviors in your repertoire, should relieve fear and tension enough to allow for a fighting chance and the beginnings of confidence on the hole.

Gambling shots create a similar situation to jinx holes because of their potential connection with failure. The amount of confidence and immunity to pressure that is experienced with a gambling shot is going to be largely a function of the history of success in the particular gambling situation. That is, if the golfer has previously been successful with gambles requiring hitting the ball farther than usual, then a little pressure may actually enhance his chances of success in situations which require extra distance. If, on the other hand, the player has often failed in situations where cutting a corner on a hole is required, then she will probably be less confident in tackling corner-cutting gambles, and pressure may make disaster even more likely.

What this amounts to is success breeding success, and failure breeding failure. Said another way, people feel more confident with their strengths than with their weaknesses. So, if you can't hook the ball under normal circumstances with a wide open fairway in front of you, don't expect to confidently pull off some fantastic hook shot under the pressure of a gambling situation. On the other hand, if you normally have good length with wood shots, you may be able to more confidently go for the green over the lake on the par-five eighteenth when a birdie will seal the victory.

Gamble only when reasonably confident in your ability to pull off the shot. This confidence is most likely to occur when calling on your usual strengths and just asking for a little extra measure of those strengths at the moment.

One last thought on gambling shots: Be sure to analyze the gambling shot carefully. Just how much of the corner really needs to be cut off? How does the reward for a successful gamble compare to the penalty for failure? Are the percentages in your favor, or are you just digging a deeper hole for yourself by gambling? Are you prepared to accept the consequences? A well-thought-out gambling shot is much more likely to meet with success than one that is approached haphazardly.

"Choking"

When pressure works against a golfer, and he messes up a crucial shot, he is likely to be accused of "choking," which refers to the lump a person gets in his throat when facing potential disaster. It might be a shot over water, a critical wedge shot, or a short putt, but the effect is the same: the proverbial lump in the throat.

When a golfer feels himself choking, several things are happening at once: (1) He is visualizing the shot perfectly. Unfortunately, it's the wrong shot, the disastrous one. When the disastrous shot is subsequently hit, the visualization has proven to be very effective, just misdirected. (2) He is distracted from key fundamentals. The pressure could probably be survived if the fundamentals of the swing were not simultaneously abandoned. (3) He is preoccupied with outcome. If he exclusively focuses on the result, then the golfer is not thinking about what has to be done over the ball to create a successful shot.

One way to cope with choking is to make visualization work for you. During the pre-shot routine, focus intently on where you want the ball to go rather than where you don't want it to go. Equally important, continue the visualization momentarily with your head down after the ball is on its way. In effect, when you do look up to see the result, it will be a surprise if your intense visualization has not materialized.

Another consideration is to let the choking sensation be a cue to refocus on the fundamentals. Basically, say to yourself, "O.K., I'm under pressure. Don't think of anything else but relaxing and keeping the head down. Forget the result and be content with doing my job over the ball." You might add, "I can't totally control where the ball ends up. I can only control what I am doing here at the site of the ball. So, I'll do my job and let the result take care of itself."

*Self-Encouragement through Self-Talk**

In general, stress and pressure are created from within the person by what one says to oneself. Test taking offers a good example: Thirty students enter a classroom to take a test. Let's

*This section was adapted from the article "Talk to Yourself," by Thomas N. Dorsel. Permission *Golf Digest*, January 1988 issue. © 1994, Golf Digest/Tennis, Inc.

MENTAL SPOTLIGHT   Lesson in Handling Tough Loss: Hoch's Composure at Masters

The story is a familiar one. Two players duel head-to-head down the stretch. Finally, one player falters while the other emerges victorious.

This year at the Masters, it was Scott Hoch faltering with a missed putt in the playoff while Nick Faldo emerged the victor. We have little trouble identifying with Faldo's joy and exhilaration in his come-from-behind win. But, in contrast, Hoch's sad defeat makes us uneasy, almost as if we take it personally. Perhaps it hits a little too close to our own insecurities, as we can easily imagine ourselves in a comparable position with similar results.

How does a guy handle such a defeat? How does he react, what does he do next? How does he explain it to others? How does he explain it to himself?

First of all, I think Scott Hoch handled it quite well. In the immediate situation, he reacted with understandable disbelief, even though his putt was not an easy one. Furthermore, he made a difficult comeback putt in the face of shaken confidence, and with the tournament truly on the line at this point. Finally, he did not stomp off pouting after the final defeat, and he blamed nobody but himself for the putt that cost him the tournament.

This sportsmanlike behavior provides the first lesson to be learned from such an unfortunate incident in a player's career. You may not win the given tournament, but you can win points for your image, which, in turn, may facilitate your success over a long career.

Another thing that a player might do in defeat is look beyond the disastrous shot to all the successful shots made along the way. Hoch reported that he hadn't had a three-putt all week. That's quite remarkable play. He also made some pressure shots down the stretch just to get into the playoff. In addition, he made those pressure shots on the final nine holes while other great players were making poor decisions, mis-hitting tee and fairway shots,

and missing their own little putts along the way. These are thoughts that a wise player in Hoch's position doesn't say aloud. But such thoughts can do him a lot of good in the privacy of his own mind.

Another coping strategy would be to view a runner-up finish as one more step on the continuum of success. It's quite a nice jump for Scott Hoch to move from relative obscurity to national visibility as a contender throughout and the eventual runner-up in a major championship. All the great players have had numerous runner-up finishes, and this runner-up finish may be just a step on the way to greatness for Scott Hoch. This is, at least, an adaptive view of the circumstances.

Lastly, golf is a difficult game and the putt Scott Hoch faced on the first playoff hole was a difficult putt. There is no way around it—a short, downhill, breaking putt on the fast greens of Augusta is no gimme. Hoch made a bunch of difficult shots during the tournament, and missed some others. The playoff putt just happened to be one that he missed.

You'll notice that I have not used the word "choke" in reflecting on the events at Augusta. To blame the missed putt on choking is too simple an explanation. If he had hit his fairway shot fat, or left his first putt halfway to the hole, then maybe choking would reasonably apply. But Hoch did too many things right in the final accounting. He simply had a tough putt, and he missed it! Now, on with a promising career as a professional golfer.

As for the rest of us—relax! We'll have to agonize through many more of these dramas—hopefully. What an exciting Masters it was, even in the dreary slop of a rainy spring weekend in Georgia.

And the next time you find yourself with a pressure putt on the 18th green of your weekend match, keep in mind that your entire self-worth does not ride on the outcome of what amounts to just one more difficult putt.

assume they have all been given the same advanced notice, the same study opportunities, and have all prepared equally well for the test. The teacher is the same, the test materials are the same, and every other factor is the same for all of the students. Yet, each student experiences a different level of stress. Some are terrified, anxious, or just plain nervous; others are eager, excited, or even cocky.

If stress were based simply on the test itself, which is the same for everybody, all students would be experiencing exactly the same level of stress. But, on the contrary, the students each experience the test situation in their own unique ways. This is because each student's personal level of stress is determined not only by the test but also by what each student says to himself or herself about the test.

Put in a more general framework for any stressful situation, the formula for stress might be as follows:

Level of Stress = Event + What One Says to Oneself

Regarding the test situation above, the event is fairly constant for all the students: It's the test and all the circumstances that the students have in common regarding preparing for the test. What varies among the students is what they are saying to themselves about the test event. The terrified student is saying, justified or not, that he must pass this test or it will be the end of his career. The anxious student is saying, "What will my parents think?" The nervous person is berating herself for not having studied more (even though she may have studied as much as everybody else). On the other hand, the eager person is saying to himself, "I've studied, I'm ready, let's go!" The excited person is saying, "This is my best subject; I can't wait to see how well I do." And the cocky person is saying, "Tests are my bread and butter. I've never found a test that I couldn't master."

This may sound like simple positive thinking, but it's not. Talking to yourself in a way that relieves stress doesn't involve reciting falsehoods, which is often the case with simple positive thinking. Such "lying" to yourself will not relieve stress. The emotions are not fooled that easily.

Stress-producing self-talk involves finding the hidden truth that is in your favor in a potentially stressful situation and then reminding yourself of this favorable truth when the stress starts to mount. Extending the example above one last time, the calm test taker might say to herself that she has studied as much as everybody else and is rested, alert, and ready. If she can't do well on this test, it is unlikely anyone else will do any better. Furthermore, if she doesn't do as well as she would like, it's only one test among many and not the end of the world in any case. This calm approach to test taking exemplifies taking a potentially stressful event and bringing it into a relaxed perspective by the choice of what you say to yourself.

Golf is just another series of tests. Golfers are all trying to achieve favorable scores, playing the same game on the same courses as all other golfers. What differs among golfers are the assortment of things that they say to themselves that create differing levels of stress. Here are some specific examples:

1. *Stress-producing self-talk.* "This course is easy. If I can't play well here, I may as well give up the game."
   Stress-reducing self-talk: "No course is easy, but I may have a decent chance to play well on this shorter course."
2. *Stress-producing self-talk*: "Par is 72. Therefore, that is what I should shoot if I expect to be called a golfer."

Stress-reducing self-talk: "Par is the ideal, not the expected score for every golfer. I'd like to shoot par, but I certainly don't set it up as an absolute requirement for me to enjoy the game."

3. *Stress-producing self-talk*: "That out of bounds looks mighty threatening. I'm sure to hit my ball over there."

   Stress-reducing self-talk: "There is more fairway than out of bounds out there. Besides I naturally fade the ball, so my shot will be moving away from the trouble."

4. *Stress-producing self-talk*: "I have to get this close to the hole. It's my only chance."

   Stress-reducing self-talk: "I'd like to get it close, but even if I don't, I still have a chance to score with my short game."

5. *Stress-producing self-talk*: "Putting is the easiest part of the game. Any blockhead should be able to putt."

   Stress-reducing self-talk: "Putting is very difficult. Unless I am practicing a lot, I have to be realistic about how many putts I'm going to make."

6. *Stress-producing self-talk*: "Oh no! I'm playing the defending club champion in my opening match. This is going to be the biggest joke ever seen."

   Stress-reducing self-talk: "Opening with the club champ. This could be very interesting, and, in fact, a real opportunity. He may take me for granted and not prepare adequately. If I put in a little extra practice and just play my own game, I may surprise him. What have I got to lose? No one expects me to win. Actually the pressure is on him. He has to win and win big or it will be a moral victory for me."

7. *Stress-producing self-talk*: "Five holes down with nine to go. I may as well give up. I can't possibly win this match."

   Stress-reducing self-talk: "If I give up now, I may miss out on the biggest comeback of my life, the one that would be talked about for years. What if all the heroes of great athletic comebacks had given up right before their historic feats began? They and the rest of us would have been denied tremendous thrills. A comeback has to begin somewhere, so why not start right now with a win on the next hole. At the very least I'll see how long I can stay alive in this match and make my opponent work for his victory."

A number of things stand out in the above comparisons. (1) The stress-producing statements put unrealistic pressure on the golfer. They set the player up for failure by suggesting more than one should expect, often more than even the best touring pros would expect. At their worst, the statements are grossly inaccurate. To say that golf is easy, courses are easy, putting is easy, or that one has no chance at all is simply wrong. (2) Stress-producing statements often conjure up unnecessarily negative images. Indeed, the ball could hook out of bounds, but it could also do many other things to include ending up in the middle of the fairway. (3) Stress-reducing statements, on the other hand, are all cool and calculating. They reflect stepping back and taking an objective view of the situation rather than taking an impulsively emotional plunge into the exclusively bleak side of things. (4) Stress-reducing statements do not lie. They are the simple truths of the matter. Admittedly, the truth is sometimes hidden behind a mask of negative emotions generated by the threatening situation at hand.

Still, the favorable truths are always there. They may just require a little digging to find them.

Safeguards Against Pressure

The following are some additional ways to inoculate oneself against pressure. Just like the human body is immunized against an impending flu virus by getting inoculated in advance, golfers can similarly prepare their bodies and minds for the pressures of the golf season by preparing in advance. Here are a few suggestions:

Overlearn

Once having practiced short putts to the point where confidence abounds, practice short putts some more. Overlearning should produce extremely well-learned skills that are enhanced by pressure, as was described at the beginning of this chapter.

Create Pressure during Practice

Any practice should help in being better prepared for pressure, but practice under pressure should help even more. Remember the earlier suggestion regarding putting practice to set a requirement of 18 successful short putts in a row, or the sequence is started over again. This procedure exerts very real pressure when the seventeenth and eighteenth putts are reached.

Keep progress records while practicing, always trying to improve on the previous best. Practice with a friend, making modest wagers on various shots to add a little heat to the situation.

Play in Tournaments

There is nothing better than competition to prepare for competition. Seek out matches, little tournaments, bigger tournaments, and so forth, gradually exposing yourself to and getting used to the pressure of competition. The goal is that competition and its accompanying pressure become simply normal aspects of the game. Pressure becomes nothing unusual; it can't sneak up and shock you into choking.

Expect Opponent to Play Well

During an actual round, a little pressure-inoculation booster can be achieved by expecting success from your opponent. For example, if both you and your opponent are both looking at short putts for par, expect your opponent to make her putt. Then it won't be such a shock if she does succeed. If, on the other hand, you are praying that she misses, the pressure will only hit harder if her putt rolls in.

MENTAL SPOTLIGHT Second-round Letdown: A Weed with Many Roots in Golf's Garden

I was recently asked why competitive golfers frequently shoot poor rounds following impressive opening rounds.

This is certainly common at the amateur level of play. But even in such prestigious tournaments as the U.S. Open, it is not uncommon to see an unknown player shoot a brilliant first round only to fall well back in the pack on the second day.

There seem to be several possible explanations for this phenomenon. First of all, golf is a difficult game. It is tough to shoot one good round, much less two good rounds back-to-back. So many factors affect the outcome of a round of golf that variability in scores is to be expected. Even when players shoot consistent scores, they tend to do it in different ways—hitting greens one day, putting well the next, getting lucky another day. So one explanation for poor second rounds is that the percentages are not in one's favor regarding shooting repeated good scores.

Second, the likelihood of shooting back-to-back good scores probably varies with the calibre of player who is attempting to shoot them. The unknown, less-experienced player who shoots the best round of his life to grab the early lead in the U.S. Open is probably more likely to back off in the second round in comparison to the seasoned, tournament-hardened veteran who has been there many times before.

Third, when a tournament begins, everyone is just a part of the field. Certainly there are favorites, but it is not surprising to anyone if even a favorite is off his game and does not appear among the leaders in a given tournament. So the eyes of the viewing public are basically scanning the field during the opening round with no strong expectations. However, once someone takes the lead, all eyes shift to that person. Now the player's anonymity is gone. He is in the spotlight. This, of course, creates additional pressure which may exceed the player's optimal level of motivation and begin to interfere with his performance.

Fourth, while some would interpret the poorer score in the second round as the player letting down, I think that the more likely explanation is that the player has gotten too excited, is expecting too much of himself, and is trying to extend himself too far beyond his initial success. Instead, the player should be staying with the strategy and skills that resulted in his good start in the first place.

A related issue to the poor-second-round phenomenon is the difficulty in defending a championship from one year to the next. Again, I think the notion of expectations plays a major role. Before you win, no one, including yourself, is expecting much of you. But after you are the champ, everyone's expectations rise. To compound the problem, you might experience the additional pressure of feeling you have to prove your first victory wasn't luck.

Of course, there are many other variables that make it difficult to defend a championship. The tournament may be held on a different course that is not as well suited to the player's game, the field may be stronger, and, perhaps most importantly, it is a year later and your game may not be quite as sharp for any number of reasons. Lord knows how our games can vary from day to day, not to mention from year to year.

Still, there are those players who do string together the consistent good scores, and who do successfully defend championships. They are the expert players who consistently practice the physical and psychological components of the game, play a lot of competitive golf, and prepare themselves for the very situations that are the focus of this article.

So, if you want to learn to have repeated good scores, make that a focus of your attention this spring. See if you can keep your scores within a consistent, narrow range, even if it means foregoing some of your usual more risky attempts at spectacular shots and rounds. If you want to learn to defend championships, start by defending smaller accomplishments, like beating your regular playing partners weekend after weekend. Make them sick of the fact that you always seem to win, week after week. Set your goals, keep them in focus, and practice, practice, practice. Golf is not a game of magic!

Allow for a Second Chance

If you find yourself being tentative, overly conservative, "playing scared" in a tournament, look into the future and imagine that the tournament is already over and you have not done well at all. Now, come back to the present and approach the remaining holes like you have just been awarded a second chance. What is there to lose by playing aggressively? You've already lost it (in your imagination) by playing scared. It can't be any worse this time around. So give it another shot, and this time play more aggressively.

Similar thinking might be useful with a lead in a match and the temptation to play overly safe while the lead dwindles away. Think of it this way: If you "safely" play yourself out of the lead, you are going to have to charge to get the lead back. So why not charge now, while you have a few strokes cushion, instead of waiting until you have fallen behind in the match?

Applying Pressure

Psychological principles are primarily intended for helping golfers deal with pressure for the purpose of improving their own games. However, there may be times in competition where it is advantageous to apply a little pressure to one's opponent, which is quite appropriate as long as it doesn't violate good sportsmanship. Cranford (1961) provided the basis for many of the suggestions which follow:

Make Your Opponent Feel Helpless

Make your opponent give up because of painful losses, hole after hole, over which he feels he has no control. A good example of how to do this would be to develop an excellent short game. When long-driving opponents face loss after loss because of your "miraculous" chips and putts, their feelings of helplessness will be evident in their mournful cries: "What can I do?" or "This guy is unconscious!"

Frustrate Your Opponent

One source of frustration is the blocking of expected reward. If your opponent is expecting the reward of being the long driver in the match, she might find it particularly frustrating if you were to outdrive her occasionally. Or if your opponent is a tremendous putter, put in some extra practice on putting so as to deprive him of the usual satisfaction he has come to expect on the greens. If your opponent has a reputation for being a strict rule caller, brush up on the rules beforehand so as not to be caught or, even better, to be able to correct your well-studied opponent should she cite one incorrectly.

Make Your Opponent Match Your Shot

Or as Cranford put it, "Shove a good shot in his face and let him do better" (p. 137). Welcome any opportunity to hit first. Concentrate extra hard and produce a successful shot, which will require your opponent to hit a shot of the highest quality just to keep up.

Situations in which the privilege of hitting first automatically occur are after winning the previous hole or when your ball rests farther from the hole than the ball of your opponent. A less obvious time that allows control over hitting first is when it comes to putting out, rather than marking the ball following your first putt on a hole. If you feel like you can give your opponent a successful putt to match, go ahead and putt it out. On the other hand, if you feel like the outcome of your putt might be in doubt, it may be wiser to mark the ball, letting your opponent assume you are likely to make the putt.

Keep the Ball in Play

Even when you are so far behind that the hole or match seems "already lost," if you keep the ball in play and stay as close as possible, your opponent will have to continue to play well in order to win the "already-won" hole or match. One or two false moves on his part, and you may be back in the thick of it. Never give your opponent a hole or match. Make him finish it off, which can sometimes be very difficult, especially when the opposition is tenacious.

Chapter *10*

Strategy, Concentration, and Imagery

Prior to the 1979 PGA Championship, a slumping Tom Watson reportedly said, "If I could just concentrate on one thing, I think I'd be all right, but I'm thinking of too many things and I'm kind of confused. . . . My thinking on the course is disorganized." Later the same year, in reference to her brilliant first- and second-year performance on the LPGA Tour, Nancy Lopez suggested that her swing wasn't really that good, and that her game was mostly mental. The statements of these star performers provide testimony that thinking plays a big part in one's golfing success.

While the thinking and physical processes of golf have been interwoven throughout the preceding chapters, the present chapter focuses exclusively on three aspects of thinking: strategy, concentration, and imagery. Each of these elements of thinking is distinctly psychological but must ultimately be combined with the physical in order to achieve golfing success.

Strategy

Superior shot-making ability does not always translate into a good score. In other words, a golfer can swing well without scoring well, and vice versa. To learn the two separate skills, Jack Nicklaus has wisely recommended that golfers devote practice to each of them. Thus, the basic principle of learning applies again: You learn what you practice.

The distinction between swinging the club and shooting a good score is not unlike many others in life. For example, a similar contrast can be made between "learning" in school and "getting good grades." Sometimes students feel as if they are learning a great deal, but without the practice of certain test-taking skills and a little academic politics, they may achieve lower grades than expected. Another example might be the distinction between working hard and making money. Tremendously hard workers abound who have made very little money in their lives. On the other hand, some laid-back individuals who seem to work less hard have made fortunes. The lesson here is that hard work must also be efficient, channeled, and well planned in order to reap the benefits of monetary gain.

In each of the above cases, two skills are involved. Both skills must be practiced and learned if a person is to experience an overall goal of succeeding at both.

The mechanics of a good swing might be practiced on the driving range or on the course without regard for score. Scoring, on the other hand, requires playing regularly, particularly competitively, and practicing the thinking that goes along with scoring well. Otherwise, one might swing flawlessly and still make stupid mistakes because of not being in the habit of thinking about the percentage shot or strategy required under various golfing circumstances.

Nicklaus's wisdom in this regard reminds me of the humorous adage: *Old age and treachery will overcome youth and skill.* While the young lions are out on the driving range perfecting the mechanics of the swing, the crusty old veterans with their creaky swings are out on the course intensely involved in a pressurized money match. And even though the dominance of golf by young collegians is well documented, sometimes the treacherous old veterans of the pressurized scoring wars emerge victorious over the youthful golfing machines, especially when the pressure is on and the score is the only thing that counts.

Scoring requires a strategy, a game plan. As introduced in Chapter Seven, a game plan includes the choice of clubs to be used on various holes, a strategy for negotiating certain hazards, a method for dealing with inclement weather, and the particular swing thoughts to focus on during the round.

Here are a few additional strategic considerations that go beyond the basic game plan and in the direction of making one a truly sophisticated, thinking player who scores well.

Playing Aggressively

Golf is meant to be fun. Fearing mistakes is not fun. Nor is it fun to play timidly, tiptoeing around the golf course scared to make a move. Fun stems from great shots, winning matches, "going for the gold."

A few years ago, I had an interesting experience of this sort. One evening near dusk I was out practicing when a few golfing buddies gathered around. "Let's play a few holes," one fellow said. "How 'bout if we play birdie or nothing," another suggested. "Forget about bogies and pars—you have to make birdie to win!" So, off we went, a foursome of seven to 11 handicappers, with gleams in our eyes and nothing but birdies in our sights.

As a member of this gang of four, I witnessed a most interesting phenomenon over the six holes that were completed before darkness set in. What impressed me was not the absolute number of birdies that were made but rather the overall elevation in the level of play that occurred.

Specifically, for the combined 24 holes the group played, 21 greens were hit in regulation, two birdies were made, a 35-foot putt lipped out denying one player of another birdie, at least eight more birdie putts were nearly made, and a combined even-par score was recorded for the foursome for the 24 holes played. Not bad, considering that the average score for any 24 holes of golf played by a foursome of seven to 11 handicappers should be in excess of 12 to 14 over par. Clearly, going for birdies raised the overall level of play a significant notch or two.

If the above is any example, playing aggressively might be a preferred strategy during regular 18-hole rounds as well. The legendary Arnold Palmer made a career of charging the hole. Consider what it might do for you:

1. Fun and excitement. When visions of Herculean feats are entertained, the game takes on a thrill of adventure. Instead of sneaking down the first fairway in hopes that the course and all of its pitfalls will leave you alone, you charge toward the green with the confidence of an epic adventurer. Instead of dreading being on the green and having to putt (maybe three times) again, you can't wait to get to the putting surface because it is there that the best opportunity to score exists. "Let me at it, another crack at success, I can't wait to see how many birdies I can make!"

2. Positive images. When it is birdie or nothing, you may as well forget about the dangers that lurk out there or the bad shots that might be hit. There's no holding back. Tentativeness is not in your vocabulary. If you expect to be in this game, only great shots are going to provide a chance. So great shots are all that are pictured in your mind.

3. Concentration. One hole, one shot at a time. You don't birdie courses, you birdie holes. Therefore, concentration is on one hole at a time. Even more importantly, the focus is intently on each individual shot. Every shot counts when trying to make a birdie. One bad shot and you might be out of the running. If you miss the green, the focus is even more intense, because now the only chance to make birdie is to knock it in the hole from off the green. Precise shots, which come from intense concentration, are the order of the day.

4. Pressure is mitigated. In an ironic twist, since there is pressure on all shots, no one shot stands out as a pressure shot. The pressure is spread out evenly over the whole round, and a tolerance is built up for it. No one shot is likely to make you choke, as might be the case when a clutch shot is suddenly needed in an otherwise casual round.

5. Comeback potential. In the event that you do get over par during the round, there is nothing to worry about. That's because the *birdie mentality* is in effect. It is easy when playing conservatively to get over par and feel like those strokes are lost forever. But since you are thinking "birdie," there is always potential for a comeback. In fact, birdie comebacks can be more thrilling than a string of steady pars.

Can a golfer be too bold? Indeed, sometimes players are criticized for being too bold, going for it when it is unnecessary. Certainly, there is a time for being conservative, or "playing smart," as golfers have come to call it. For example, when all that is needed is two putts from 15 feet to win the match, even the most aggressive player would consider it foolish to charge the hole trying to finish with one putt.

Yet, even with a lead in the match, playing safe and conservative may not always be the smartest alternative. If the situation presents an opportunity for an aggressive knockout of your opponent, or if conservative play may leave your opponent with a potential advantage, or if you are a player who simply has difficulty backing off, then playing conservatively may work against you. You may start unwittingly giving away strokes. In this case, there may be no other choice but to play an aggressive game.

MENTAL SPOTLIGHT   Floyd's Boldness in Playoff Sensible under Circumstances

You have to have been in contention in a few tournaments yourself, or at least have had a few uncomfortable bets late in a round, to be able to appreciate what Raymond Floyd was going through during his final holes in the 1990 Masters.

As for me, when Ray was walking up the eighteenth fairway at Augusta on a late Sunday afternoon looking at getting down in two from the trap to tie Nick Faldo in regulation, my chest was tight, there was a hollow feeling in my stomach, my palms were sweating, and I was generally in a state of anxiety that surely rivaled Floyd's in quality, if not quantity. I'm sure many of you experienced the same sensations.

The commentators kept saying, and even Raymond himself insisted prior to the round, that he was just out there to enjoy himself. I don't believe it! One can't afford the distraction of enjoying oneself under such competitive circumstances.

Can you imagine someone in Floyd's shoes allowing himself the luxury of thinking, "Here I am at age 47, a commanding lead on the back nine on Sunday at Augusta. The weather and playing conditions are ideal, the gallery is behind me, I'm playing great, and I feel on top of the world. At my age this may be my last chance to experience this, so I'm going to really enjoy it."

Baloney!

You can't afford to think like that. You have to block all that out and stay focused on the task at hand. I'm sure that is what Raymond actually did, even though he was engaging in a little "enjoyment" self-talk to moderate the understandable stress of the situation.

Certainly Floyd's skill, experience and ability to concentrate under pressure enabled him to survive the eighteenth in regulation. There, he twice came out of bunkers to save par and force the sudden death showdown with Faldo.

But, then, the playoff.

It is easy to be critical of Floyd for boldly going for the pin on the second playoff hole, with the resulting shot landing in the pond to the left of the green, all but effectively ending the tournament at that point.

But what choice did he really have?

Consider the following: Floyd was hitting first to the green, with no way to know how successful Faldo would be on his subsequent approach shot. If Ray decided to hit it safely out to the right of the pin, and Nick then stuck his ball in close with his short-iron approach, Ray would be kicking himself for playing it safe. As it turned out, Floyd decided on the alternative strategy, to go for the pin, and ended up kicking himself for his boldness and the resulting shot in the hazard.

Either way he was running the risk of a strategic error. He chose to chance it on the side of boldness. This seems understandable since conservative play might be blamed for the squandering of his earlier advantage on the back nine in regulation play. He certainly didn't want to give away the playoff in the same manner.

Just like last year with Scott Hoch, we can only guess what was going through Ray Floyd's mind as he watched the Masters slip away. And just like last year, we have to hand it to Nick Faldo for his cool and tenacious pursuit of victory. Like Hoch in 1989, Floyd did not lose in 1990. He confronted a formidable task, rose to the occasion time and again, and handled himself admirably, both as a player and as a person, in the process.

In the end, however, Nick Faldo simply won the golf tournament, with some great play and poise of his own.

Scrambling

If golfers play aggressively, they will probably find themselves in trouble periodically. Aggressive players must be prepared to scramble, which refers to making a good score on a hole despite any difficulties that are encountered. Scrambling can be as simple as when a player's second shot barely misses the green on a par-four hole, thereby requiring a good chip and one putt to par the hole. Scrambling can also be as complex as when a drive lands behind a tree on a par-three hole, the second shot goes into a bunker, the sand shot travels well past the hole, and then the day is saved by knocking in a 30-foot putt for a bogey.

Scrambling is something the mind must be strategically prepared for. When Arnold Palmer was making his fabled birdie barrages back in the 1960s, he knew he was going to get into some trouble because of his aggressive play. But he was mentally prepared for it when it happened. That's why he was not only a birdie machine but also a great scrambler. It was all part of his strategy.

Another way to look at it is that golf is not a game of perfection but rather an exercise in surviving imperfection. Good rounds are often built on avoiding disastrous holes rather than on making birdie after birdie. To save bogey from what could have easily been a triple bogey can often be as thrilling as making a birdie.

To give a personal example, one day I was in the process of chopping up a difficult par four on the course I usually play. After hitting a tree on the drive and hooking a 2 iron behind a large bush by a creek, I found the ball lying about 140 yards from the green. My problems weren't over, however, because the ball was completely stymied; i.e., blocked from further direct progress. The only play, at first glance, was a shot laterally into the fairway, which still would have left the ball 140 yards from the green with a difficult pin placement for the next shot. Staring at a very possible seven on this par-four hole, I decided to try a more exciting, if not the wisest, alternative. The obstructing bush had a hint of thinness to it that made me wonder if I couldn't choke down on a 2 iron and ram it low, through the thinnest part of the bush. I thought that even if I encountered a few branches, I would have enough power on the 2 iron to end up on the other side of the bush, which would be no worse than hitting the shot sideways into the fairway. So, I smacked it fairly cleanly through the bush, it rolled up near the green, and I was left with an easy pitch and a putt for a bogey. Turning that possible seven into a five went a long way toward achieving a respectable score, and it was an exhilarating moment in its own right.

Now I'm not recommending going around like Don Quixote attacking every tree, bush, and windmill on the golf course. The point is simply that one doesn't have to be playing perfectly to have fun, or even to score well. Touring pros often seem to say that they didn't hit it well on a given day, and yet posted very competitive scores. Indeed, scrambling seems to be very much in fashion these days when one considers all the acclaim that is awarded such touring pros as Ballesteros and Crenshaw for their heroic recovery shots. In fact, the touring pros who are hitting the most greens in regulation are only averaging between 12 and 13 greens per round. So, there must be an awful lot of scrambling going on out there.

And why not? Gambling, scrambling, recovering, and occasionally achieving the nearly impossible are all fun, as well as skillful. Golf would be dull without them. Admittedly, an occasional round of trouble-free pars would be refreshing now and again. But it is also permissible to be off your game on a given day and get into a bit of trouble. It may just be your day to be a scrambler, a survivor, a master of the recovery shot. Won't it be fun to sit around the clubhouse and hear your partners lamenting your miraculous recoveries?

Damage Control

Try as one may, sometimes scrambling efforts are going to be unsuccessful and a hole is going to get away from the golfer. Once again, golf is more a game of managing mistakes than of producing great shots. Achieving the greatness of a touring pro will admittedly require great shots. But for those who are trying to merely survive amateur rounds, more suffering comes from triple bogies that didn't have to happen than from birdies that got away.

It is not uncommon for weekend golfers to get to the course just before their tee times, fail to warm up, rush off the first tee, and destroy the first few holes in the process. By the fourth hole, the round is pronounced ruined, and these dejected players proceed to go through the motions for the next four hours with little enjoyment and even less productive performance. Thus, the first rule regarding managing mistakes is: Warm up, review swing thoughts, and give yourself a chance to survive the first few holes. Don't create unnecessary mistakes at the beginning of a round.

Even with this precaution, however, the first few holes are likely to be a struggle. Don't let them get out of control. If you find yourself in a little trouble off the first tee, play it safe and ensure a bogey. Don't attempt some miraculous recovery shot before getting adequately loosened up and into your rhythm. The result could easily be a double or triple bogey and a long climb back to a respectable score.

But let's say that you do find yourself heading for a double bogey on the third hole. It's a difficult par 4, you're behind a tree on the drive, you chip out safely, but still find your ball a long way from the green. You're thinking that you've got to put this 190-yard, long-iron shot on the green, or it's certainly a double bogey. So you get tense, force the shot, and pull it out of bounds, ending up with a buzzard (one of those unspeakable scores) on the hole. By this time you are saying to yourself, "If only I could have kept it to a double-bogey!"

Instant Replay: Let's return to the fairway after the chip from behind the tree and see how managing your mistakes might involve a different train of thought: "My third shot is still a tough one. I may not get it on the green, but I want to make sure that I leave myself a reasonable chip if I don't. That way I still may be able to chip it close and make a putt for bogey. Who knows, I may even chip it in; or even if the chip is poor, I may knock in a long putt. The one thing I do know is that I won't have any chance for recovery if I go for broke on this long iron and knock it out of bounds. So let's hit a percentage shot."

But, suppose that despite this calculated thinking, you still depart the third green with a double bogey on the scorecard. Not only that, you're four over par after three holes, leaving you with the option of either writing this round off as a waste, or choosing a more constructive way of looking at it. The constructive option could begin by consoling yourself that the hole was, at least, kept to a double bogey, as opposed to turning into a total disaster. You could follow this thought by challenging yourself to get your first par of the day on the next hole, rather than trying to get it all back in one hole and possibly creating more trouble. (As one wise golfer put it: Don't try to follow a bad shot with a *great* shot; just follow it with a *good* shot.) You could remind yourself that a few pars in a row would put you right back in striking distance of a respectable front nine. An unexpected birdie or two could really go a long way toward turning things around. But all this is possible only if you hang in there and keep plugging away.

But, once again, consider the less than perfect scenario: You struggle and make the turn in 43, unacceptable for someone who expects to shoot in the 70s. What can be done now to salvage the day? Obviously, you are not playing as well as you like. But can the round somehow be kept respectable? A good back nine could still produce a round in the 70s. But even a 40 would keep you in the low 80s. If the low 80s is the poorest score you ever shoot when having a bad day, that's an accomplishment in itself. However, to let an 83 turn into a 90 is to give up and run from the challenge of the game. Golf not only presents the challenge of turning good scores into great scores when playing well. It also presents the challenge of keeping bad scores from becoming terrible scores when playing poorly.

Golf can be unforgiving, but it can also be merciful; and it seems to be more merciful on those who keep trying. Golf affords multiple chances. If an approach shot is not successful, the chip shot may be. If the chip goes astray, a long putt may find the hole. And even if the long putt is not well struck, a bogey can still be salvaged with an accurate six- or seven-foot putt. Three recovery opportunities in one hole! Multiply that by 18, and an estimate of a round's worth of "second chances" is determined.

When it comes to damage control, you have to have a strategy, a set of thoughts, for coping with disaster. Know your strategy well, having rehearsed it before the actual debacle. The strategy has to be on call, as it can't be formulated in the heat of the action. Above all, remember that many a good round has survived a bad hole. What a round can't survive is giving up. Hang in there. Even surviving can be fun.

Comfort Range

Related to scrambling and damage control is the concept of the comfort range, which is a range of scores within which a given golfer's scores tend to fall, a level of play which the golfer has come to expect and feels comfortable with, a range which reflects the golfer's typical or average performance. Using statistical terminology, the comfort range might comprise an average score with a standard deviation of two or three.

The importance of the comfort range is that it may subtly affect performance on the golf course. That is, when a golfer's performance on a given day strays too far from the comfort range, the level of play tends to be modified to bring the performance back into the expected range. If the golfer is shooting better than usual, she may get tense and create some mistakes (perhaps, unconsciously) to raise her score. If the golfer is shooting worse than usual, she may relax (give up?) or bear down a bit, either of which may bring her performance back in line.

Is the comfort range just a myth, or is there some scientific foundation for this theoretical concept? To explain the comfort zone, mathematicians would likely call upon the concept of central tendency, which is the tendency for a group of scores to gather around a central point, or average, as in the normal, bell-shaped curve. To the extent that 18 holes of golf provide a group of scores, the score on any given hole might be expected to tend toward the overall scoring average for holes, in general. Similarly, scores for any given round might tend toward the golfer's average for all scores over the years.

Another explanation for the comfort zone might come from social psychologists, whose theory of cognitive dissonance proposes that consistency in life is preferred. When inconsistency is experienced by a person's thinking one way, but behaving another, psychological discomfort arises. An attempt to relieve the discomfort is made by modifying either the thoughts or the behavior in the direction of consistency.

For example, it is inconsistent for a golfer to be thinking, "I am an 85-shooter," while watching himself make 5 pars in a row. One way to achieve consistency would be to throw in a double bogey or two, which would put him right back on track to his usual 80 to 90 comfort range.

Another way to achieve consistency would be for the golfer to quit thinking, "I'm an 85-shooter," and start thinking, "I'm a 75-shooter." But this type of thinking isn't as easy as firing off a pair of double bogeys.

People tend to cling to their self-images. For example, many fat people who achieve thinness have a hard time thinking of themselves as actually thin. Instead, they think of themselves as formerly fat people who happen to look a little thinner at the moment. Similarly, 85-shooters have a hard time thinking of themselves as 75-shooters, even if they are running off a series of pars and birdies. Instead, they tend to think of themselves as 85-shooters who have been temporarily lucky. People like to validate their self-concepts, even if those self-concepts are unflattering. Perhaps this makes life less confusing, or, at least, more consistent.

So, is there no hope for improving one's golf scores? Are scores doomed to fall within the comfort range? Is it out of the question to lower the comfort range?

Lowering one's comfort range is a difficult task, but it can be accomplished if it is done gradually. In a sense, it has to be approached unawares. Consider that the comfort range develops very rationally. It forms its range based on a long history of scores. If over the years it experiences scores typically between 80 and 90, then that is the range it will encompass. It is not going to change because a given score falls considerably outside this range very rarely.

But if the comfort range starts consistently seeing a few scores just outside of its limits, say in the 77–79 range, the comfort range can quite readily accommodate to this reasonable demand. In other words, the comfort range can't be expected to change too much, too fast, but it will adjust gradually to consistent, small expansions of its scoring limits.

What this says to the golfer is to aim for gradual improvement. Look for small gains, not quantum leaps. First try to consistently shoot scores at the lower end of the comfort range (e.g., low 80s for the 85-shooter), while occasionally cutting off another stroke or two on better days. Most importantly, don't let rounds get away on the high side. If a series of good holes is followed by a double bogey or two, don't say, "Here we go again," and then let it slip away to 90 or 95. Instead, view it as a day that may require struggling a bit to keep the score away from the upper end of the comfort range.

Another thing to consider when a run of good holes occurs is not to get too excited. Keep it in perspective. Avoid thoughts of a potentially outstanding score. Instead, concentrate on the mechanics that are creating the present success. Tell yourself, "I can't totally control my score, but I can continue to keep my head down on each and every shot." Good scores will follow from good mechanics consistently applied over the entire 18 holes.

When it comes to the comfort zone, the old "good news bad news" routine applies aptly. The bad news is that it won't help to tell yourself what a good golfer you are. You have to *show* yourself, because the comfort range knows the truth. The good news is that all golfers can probably shoot a few strokes better than is presently the case. This requires a little more concentration on fundamental mechanics, not giving stokes away unnecessarily, and not expecting quantum leaps of improvement.

Keep your future rounds at or below your present average score. Whenever possible, scratch and claw out a few more pars to put your score just below the comfort range. By doing this, the comfort range will have to shift lower, because the present average can't be maintained if you don't shoot any more scores at or above it.

The comfort zone relates to scrambling and damage control, because the easiest way to lower one's average level of play is by not wasting strokes, which is accomplished by scrambling and damage control. This is a strategic consideration that has to be planned for, because golfers never know when "one of those days" is going to descend upon them.

Concentration and "The Zone"

All the pros swing differently. Many have graceful, smooth swings, with a long backswing and an even longer follow through. Others have more compact swings, appearing to punch the ball with an intense, abbreviated stroke. Some swings are fast, some are slow. Some fade the ball, others favor a draw.

But the swings of all accomplished golfers have one thing in common: they are the same through the hitting area. The hitting area is that portion of the 360-degree swing arc which comprises about 45 degrees (or two feet) on each side of the ball. It seems that equally proficient swings use different amounts of the entire 360-degree arc and meander through a variety of different directions on the backswing and follow through. Still, they all achieve a common swing position through the hitting area.

Just as the swings of the pros differ, their psychological approaches to the game differ, also. But, again, there are certain psychological fundamentals that all successful pros seem to adhere to, a sort of psychological "hitting area."

First, they have the ability to *concentrate intently*. Successful pros know what they need to focus on, blocking out all distractions in the process. Lee Trevino, reflecting on his humorous antics on the golf course, was quoted as saying, "I can't concentrate for five hours; I'd go crazy. I just need five seconds to tap my foot and hit it. But I'm very serious for those five seconds." Those very serious five seconds that Trevino refers to are an example of intent concentration.

Second, the pros' concentration focuses on certain *fundamentals and swing keys*. Although the pros know the basics of grip, stance, and body position, there are times when they have to concentrate intently on one or another of these fundamentals. At other times, their concentration might be directed toward some swing key that is peculiar to their own personal game. Swing keys might include certain internal verbalizations such as "slowing it down" or some form of mental imagery such as Nicklaus's imagining that his putter shaft is made out of delicate, blown glass. The fundamental or swing key may change from time to time, but whatever it is, that is what the successful golfer concentrates on.

Third, the accomplished professionals *practice concentrating* on those fundamentals or swing keys, so that they can be repeated throughout an entire 18-hole round. Most amateurs can concentrate on something for a few holes. But it is difficult to maintain concentration for an entire round. The pros must persevere for 18 holes, and they achieve this only from practice, practice, practice.

What this suggests for you is to isolate fundamentals that you must focus on and personal swing keys that work particularly for you. Then, make it the primary objective of each shot to intently concentrate on those fundamentals or swing keys. Don't base your success solely on the outcome of the shot. Base it equally as much on whether or not you achieved concentration on your swing key. Furthermore, if you achieve successful concentration on the key elements of the swing, successful outcomes will surely follow.

Stretch the ability to concentrate by practicing it over and over again. See if you can extend concentration further into the round than you have previously. Consider it a step in the right direction if you maintain concentration through eight holes instead of the seven with which you were successful last time. And if you do lose concentration at some point, try to get it back for another run of holes during the remainder of the round.

I once tested this approach to concentration by picking one thing, and only one thing, to concentrate on intensely for 18 holes. I chose *seeing the clubhead pass smoothly through the ball* as the thing I would make sure to do on every shot. I avoided making a primary concern out of where the ball might go or what my score might be on any given hole. The only goal was to see the clubhead pass smoothly through the ball on every shot.

As an eight handicapper at the time on a par-71 course, I could expect to shoot 79 or better on a fourth of all my rounds. My best score on this course had been a 77. Now, armed with my same old game, but with the added dimension of intent concentration, I headed off the first tee once again.

The result was eight pars and a scrambling bogey in the first nine holes. On the back side, five pars out of the first six holes leaving me only two over par with three holes to go. At this point golfing humanity re-emerged and I thought: "Look out, you're in striking distance of a good score!" My intent concentration faltered, and I went three over par on the next two holes before I could re-group and par the eighteenth for a 76. But, how about that? A guy who regularly struggles for 79s, whose best ever on the course was a 77, now falters to a 76, after being in very realistic striking distance of a 73 or 74!

Of course, many factors could have contributed to the lower score, but intense concentration was the only one that was consciously added. I kept a record while playing of how many times I actually did what I was trying to do—that is, *see the clubhead pass smoothly through the ball*. It tabulated to 86 percent of the shots.

Continued efforts with intent concentration were correlated with a 25 percent drop in my handicap from eight to six at the time. This meant that my old best became a fairly routine score.

It's likely that intent concentration is what made the legendary players great. Hogan was renowned for being unlikely to recognize his mother while he was in the middle of a round due to his intent concentration. In our own time, the faces and demeanor of players like Palmer, Player, and Nicklaus provide good reflections of intent concentration.

Certainly everyone isn't going to shoot 65 simply by concentrating. But you may get the most out of what you are capable of if you add this dimension to your game.

Full-focus

The following are some suggestions for facilitating the ability to concentrate throughout an entire 18-hole round. Such mental endurance is quite a challenge which requires planning, just like every other aspect of golf.

1. Segment the round. Considerable effort is required to remain fully focused for 18 consecutive holes. But it may be possible to fool your mind by committing it to concentrate for only three holes at a time. That is, instead of playing an 18-hole round, play a series of six three-hole rounds, beginning concentration anew with each segment. Before your mind realizes it, concentration may have occurred for the majority of the 18-hole round.

Keep a record of the number of three-hole segments during which concentration was achieved. Don't base success solely on the outcome of the shot or the scores on the holes. Base success equally as much on whether or not concentration was achieved over the various 3-hole spans.

2. Review swing thoughts periodically. The swing thought may be some mechanical aspect of the swing (e.g., slow down the backswing), some verbalization that encourages proper tempo (e.g., back-and-through), or some visualization that makes the swing flow with balance and power (e.g., imagining the ball exploding off the clubface and knocking down the flagstick). Whatever the swing thought is, don't just start off with it and then let it slide into the recesses of your mind somewhere between the sixth and twelfth hole. It's easy to think you are still concentrating on the swing thought when actually you're not. Instead, your primary focus may have shifted to score, the trouble you're getting into, or casual conversation with your playing companions.

In order to maintain vital concentration on swing thoughts, periodically the swing thoughts need to be intensely reviewed, and the best time for this review is on the practice swing. Say the key elements to yourself, intently concentrating on each aspect of the swing thought as you take the practice swing.

3. Don't panic. While the goal is to concentrate for the entire round, the greater likelihood is that a lapse in concentration is likely to occur somewhere during the round. Don't fall apart at these times. Remember, golf is not a game of perfection. Rather, it is a game of surviving imperfection.

When you have emerged from the inevitable bad shot, or bad hole, or even shaky stretch of holes, get off by yourself and pause for a moment, refocus on your swing thought, and make a commitment to another stretch of concentration.

When touring pro Gary Player misses a shot, he stands over to the side taking slow, deliberate practice strokes, which surely constitute a review of the swing thought that has just escaped him. He is correcting it in his mind immediately. Such momentary lapses of concentration are not times to hang crepe, but merely times for a little damage control. Above all, don't panic; merely refocus and press on with a renewed sense of challenge and even greater commitment to concentrate on your swing thought.

4. Keep goals flexible. Modifying goals as dictated by the circumstances of the round may help you regain lost concentration. When a round is in distress, focus on the next three-hole segment as an opportunity to begin a great comeback. As described previously, remind yourself that some of the greatest thrills in sports have been the nearly impossible comebacks. This may be *your* time, and you surely don't want to miss it by giving up. If nothing else, here is a chance to add another successful three-hole segment to your records.

Regressing a bit, a goal for the beginning of a round might be to achieve successful concentration for the first three holes. That is, the focus is simply on making a good start. Of course, if a good start is achieved, the momentum has a good chance of carrying over into the rest of the round. The important thing is that a bit of the pressure has been relieved by the initial commitment of concentrating for only the first three holes.

Another beginning goal might be to see how many holes can be played before losing concentration, and to see if that number can be increased a little each round. If it was seven holes yesterday, let's see if it can be eight holes today. If you lose it, start another run of holes for the remainder of the round. The count can even continue into the next round, which means a new run at your personal record can begin at any point in the round, even on the last hole.

A goal for the end of any round, particularly for a round that has gotten away from you, is to make a solid finish. Pretend the last three holes are not those of the present debacle, but rather the finale of some future round in which a strong finish is crucial. Can you do it? Apply a little pressure. Such mind games should enhance your ability to concentrate and provide some valuable practice at putting the finishing touches on all of your rounds.

5. Socialize, but don't blame others for your errors. Playing companions and spectators are a source of fun and enjoyment in golf, but they are also a source of distraction that must be contended with. It is the golfer's responsibility to concentrate despite distractions from outside agents.

Consider the distracting conditions under which touring pros play. If they stopped constantly to calm the crowd, chastise spectators, or lament misfortune that can emanate from these circumstances, they would not only create more distractions for themselves, they would never finish a round.

How do the pros handle distractions? For one thing, they regularly expose themselves to chaotic conditions with the result that concentration is extensively practiced in the face of distraction. It therefore doesn't come as such a shock to them when chaos occurs. Also, they do not allow themselves the easy way out of blaming others when failure occurs. If they miss a shot, they accept it as their fault for not concentrating intently enough. And lastly, the pros do things to avoid distractions, such as Ballesteros having his caddie serve as a shield between him and the ever-moving gallery, or Trevino hitting his shot quickly before Arnie's Army (the extensive gallery that follows Arnold Palmer) sounds off for their hero as he approaches an adjacent hole. Fourth, some pros even use distractions to their advantage, such as Chi Chi Rodriguez and Fuzzy Zoeller who cut up with the gallery as a means of relaxing. As described earlier, Lee Trevino combines antics with the crowd with intent concentration when he says, "I can't concentrate for five hours; I'd go crazy. I just need five seconds to tap my foot and hit it. *But I'm very serious for those five seconds.*" Again, it's that serious five seconds which is the intent concentration that is necessary for superior golf.

In concluding this discussion, the key thing about concentration is to pick some small element of the situation and focus on it at the expense of everything else. If it's a dot on the ball, then focus on that dot and forget about any other aspect of the ball, green, or hole. If it's a very specific target, intently gaze at that target and eliminate all other environmental features from your visual field. If it is a specific swing thought, make absolutely sure to execute that swing thought, and do it with no concern for the outcome of the shot.

The only additional ingredient is to take quick and decisive action. This does not mean to rush, but simply not to dally, waste time, or second-guess yourself. The length of time

MENTAL SPOTLIGHT   The Zone

Finding the "Zone." Pros talk about it, amateurs fantasize about it, but does anyone really know what it is?

Lacking a definition in Webster's, I would say that the Zone involves three elements: (1) very positive images; (2) an ultra-relaxed state; and (3) an extremely clear focus on swing thoughts. The combination of these creates a "can't miss" attitude that leads to outstanding performance over a period of time. The Zone never lasts as long as we'd like, but you should ride it for all it's worth when it happens.

That's another thing about the Zone—it just "happens."

For example, you're three over, as usual, when you get to the par-three fourth hole. Out of nowhere, your tee shot drops next to the pin and you make birdie. On the fifth, you hit another spectacular approach for another easy bird. You're feeling, "How can I miss?" and even if you do miss a green, you know you'll get it up and down. That is, if you don't chip it in.

If you have a hard time imagining this scenario, consider the opposite—a rut of bad holes when you can't make anything, when all you see are images of disaster and par seems unattainable.

The Zone is the flip side of that broken record. It is a positive rut that flows from a few spectacular shots. Playing well leads to beautiful images, peaceful relaxation and intense concentration. It's been said that one's focus becomes so intense that vision seems to sharpen. As you address the ball, the logo and the dimples jump off the cover, the blades of grass are individual bristles and, most important, there's nothing in your mind but crystal-clear images of success.

If it sounds as if I'm describing a work of art, that's not far off the mark. The Zone stimulates the senses, the way poetry or a painting does. It's flamboyant, grandiose—and the shotmaking that coincides with it lives up to those expectations. At its best, the Zone is a peaceful hypnotic trance that you hate to leave.

But, unfortunately, you can't stay in the Zone forever; eventually you return to familiar reality. With any luck, you can stay in the Zone through the end of your round, but don't bet on it. Be happy you found the Zone at all.

Is there a way to bring on the Zone? Well, if it was that automatic, somebody would have bottled the formula long ago. But, although the Zone can't be turned on and off like a switch, there are ways to put yourself in position to make it happen.

Everybody has a Zone. For the tour pro, it's birdie upon birdie leading to an outrageous score in the low 60s. For the weekend amateur, the Zone may be six straight two-putt bogeys. In either case, two or three great shots in a row may get the Zone rolling.

The better player, of course, has a better chance of stringing together a few great shots and finding the Zone. Therefore, it's not only, "The more I practice, the luckier I get," but also, "The more I practice, the better my chances of finding the Zone."

You may be able to encourage the Zone with preround visualization. Between the practice area and the first tee, walk off by yourself for a few minutes and focus intensely on swing thoughts or imagine spectacular shots. It might sound a little strange, but you can even study the ball you're about to use in an effort to enhance its definition. Consciously working to heighten your senses may increase your chances of finding the Zone.

While you don't want to take foolish chances early in a round, you might entertain thoughts of great shots in the first few holes. It can't hurt to consider this possibility, and such imagery might enhance your luck.

If you're in the middle of a round that's going nowhere, shift your goal to hitting at least one great shot before you finish. Rather than going through the motions for the remainder of the round, this will give purpose to each shot, give you a point of focus and perhaps propel you into the Zone during an otherwise uneventful day.

When you do find yourself in the Zone, don't disrupt it. Don't leave the course between nines; stick with your playing partners and don't let outsiders distract you. In other words, keep a good thing going! You'll be out of the Zone soon enough, so don't accelerate the process.

By Thomas N. Dorsel, *GOLF Magazine* (October, 1991). Copyright © 1992, 1993 by *GOLF Magazine*.

that intent concentration can persist is limited to a very few seconds. Any longer, and questions, doubts, and distractions are sure to creep into your consciousness.

Imagery

One of the pithy quotes attributed to Mark Twain is, "I've had a lot of troubles in my life, most of which never happened." While we tend to imagine a lot of troubles in life that never actually come about, the situation seems to be the opposite in golf where disastrous images often come to fruition. All one has to do is imagine a ball going out of bounds, and away it goes. Line up a putt and envision it lipping out of the hole, and it's a foregone conclusion. That putt is lost before the ball is even addressed.

Positive imagery, of course, also occurs. Occasionally the line on a long putt is perfectly envisioned; it just seems like a sure thing. The ball is seen rolling in a gentle curve to the hole and disappearing gracefully over the front edge of the cup. When the putt is made, the event actually happens. A similar situation can occur on the tee of certain holes which lend themselves to an image of a perfect drive. The shot is envisioned and subsequently becomes a reality.

Perhaps the most outrageous story concerning the effectiveness of positive images is the one about a fellow many years ago who had a dream about making a hole in one on the tenth hole. After relating the dream to his fellow golfers, a number of them gathered around the tenth tee and made bets on the likelihood of the foretold event actually occurring. To everyone's amazement, the dreamer aced the hole. Could it have been that the golfer's dream created such an intensely positive image that the likelihood of the perfect shot was enhanced to the level of predictability?

How do images work? Where do they come from, how do they impact on the swing, how can they be made to work to the golfer's benefit, as opposed to detriment?

The Source of Images

Observation is probably the most potent source of images. It is, therefore, important to observe models who are successful if one is going to generate images of success. Unfortunately, the most available model on the golf course is that provided by each individual golfer watching himself, who may regularly be seen producing unsuccessful shots.

To change this detrimental observational situation, golfers must create circumstances where they see themselves performing successfully. Mastery practice, as described in Chapter Six, is ideal for accomplishing this objective. If there is a particular spot on the course where unfavorable images dominate, repeated shots should be hit from that location until enough good ones are seen that new positive images can compete with old ones of disaster.

Another way to create positive images might be observation of an accomplished golfer who is similar to the learner in such things as age, build, and style of play. This model might be a pro on the PGA Tour, or an expert amateur in the local area. Clearly, it would be nice to observe them frequently and have many opportunities to witness their successes. At the same time, a single observation can sometimes have a very powerful effect and remain imprinted on the imagination forever.

An innovative idea for creating an ideal model to observe and imitate would be to videotape a round of mastery practice, and edit out the unsuccessful attempts, leaving only the shots of a classic round of golf. In viewing this tape over and over, a golfer would see *herself* making perfect swings with perfect outcomes. There could be no better model to imagine and imitate.

The Impact of Images

There may be nothing magical about the impact of images in some cases. For example, situations arise where the line of a putt is imagined perfectly. Could it be that the correct line is truly being seen on this particular putt, and this accurate perception increases the golfer's confidence and relaxation, which in turn translates into the golfer keeping the head still and doing whatever else it takes to hit a solid putt? Rather than the image itself leading directly to a successful putt, it may be more likely that increased confidence, relaxation, and proper technique combine to produce the desired result.

On the other hand, conscious efforts at using imagery probably have a direct impact on performance in many cases. Indeed, Orlick and Partington (1988) state that 99 percent of 235 Canadian athletes who participated in the 1984 Olympic Games reported using imagery of one form or another in preparation for their events.

Vealey and Walter (1993) describe two theories of how imagery may work directly to facilitate performance. The first theory is *psychoneuromuscular theory*, which relates to golf in a manner which is commonly called "muscle memory." That is, whenever a shot is actually hit, two things are happening for the golfer: (1) Her visible body parts (arms, legs, torso, etc.) are in action, and (2) her invisible nervous system is active in a way that parallels the external movement of the body parts. When imagery occurs alone through mental practice, it may give the nervous system a "practice swing" before it has to actually perform along with the external body parts.

The second theory is *symbolic learning theory*, which may be more commonly thought of as a "mental blueprint" for the shot that is about to take place. That is, just as a building contractor likes to have a picture on paper of what he is about to build out of bricks and mortar, a golfer may benefit from having a picture in his brain of what he is about to perform with his muscles and joints. This symbolic mental representation provides an internal guideline or plan, giving the performer a little familiarity in advance regarding how to proceed.

Which Images to Use

Before formally introducing imagery to one's game, the most useful images to employ must be determined. At least three choices exist:

1. *Visual images* are what usually come to mind when golfers talk about imagery. These are mental pictures such as the ball sailing high and straight and landing softly near its target, or just a very vivid image of the target itself. One expert golfer said that he thought of nothing other than knocking down the flagstick during his swing. Palmer and Nicklaus have said things in the past that suggest their entertaining intense visual images when they play.

2. *Verbal images* are also common. These are things golfers say to themselves during the swing, usually about the mechanics of the swing, that provide an image of what is trying to be accomplished during the swing. "Big and smooooooth" or "down and through" are examples of verbal images. Or a simple reminder to keep the head down falls into this category.

3. *Kinesthetic images* are a third type of imagery that one might tap. These are visual or verbal cues that elicit a certain feeling which is conducive to a successful shot. As mentioned earlier, Nicklaus likes to think of his putter shaft as constructed of fragile glass, so as to encourage him to make a gentle, delicate stroke. Also previously described, Sam Snead suggested gripping the club lightly, as if holding a bird; i.e., not so loosely that it flies away but not so tightly that the bird is squeezed to death. Wiren and Coop (1978) provide several nice examples of this type of imagery to include "splash" for hitting out of dry sand versus "splat" for hitting out of wet sand. They also mention a golfer who used to think of the word "feathers" whenever he putted, an image that would presumably encourage the same light touch that Nicklaus accomplishes by imagining his putter has a glass shaft.

Wiren and Coop suggest another kind of kinesthetic image which they call *tempo cues*. These are series of words, often unrelated to golf, which mimic the desired tempo of the golf swing. "Ladies and Gentlemen," with the emphasis on "Gen," serves as a good example. Humming the beginning of the Danube Waltz also mimics the tempo of the backswing and the move into impact.

Which type of imagery is best for any given golfer will have to be determined by trial and error. It seems that some people have considerable difficulty generating and holding visual images but are very good with verbal cues. The opposite may be true for others. Whether the golfer is a visualizer, a verbalizer, or a kinesthizer doesn't matter, as long as it works for her.

A caution mentioned earlier is worth repeating: Once an image is firmly envisioned, the golfer should not waste any time executing the shot. No image can last forever. If a player stands around entertaining an image too long, other distractions are sure to creep in and destroy the effectiveness of an otherwise constructive image.

Imagery Practice

As early as the 1960s, evidence was provided that mental practice can be nearly as effective as physical practice. Clark (1960) compared physical practice and mental practice on foul shot improvement in basketball. The physical practice group actually practiced shooting foul shots while the mental practice group merely imagined shooting foul shots. When tested after using their respective practice procedures for a couple of weeks, the mental practice group was found to have improved almost as much as the physical practice group. The effect was particularly dramatic for experienced players in comparison to novice players, which suggests that a certain amount of physical experience may be necessary to achieve maximal benefit from mental practice.

In golf, mental imagery practice may be beneficial during the off season as well as between rounds. An equally important opportunity for mental rehearsal is on the way to the course before a round. Instead of waiting until reaching the practice tee or the putting green to begin reviewing swing thoughts, get a head start by beginning the process while still behind the wheel of the car. Mental rehearsal should, of course, continue during pre-round warm-up, as well as between and just prior to execution of shots.

Another imagery technique which is related to practice is *anchoring* (King, Novik, and Citrenbaum, 1983). As part of a mental practice routine, retrieve from memory some great shots that you have hit during actual competition. The shots may have occurred recently, or they may be some classic shots that you have hit over the years and will never forget. As you vividly imagine the circumstances of each of those great shots (the sights, the sounds, the feelings, the results) you will notice a relaxed, confident state come over you, just the kind of state that is desirable for hitting a good shot at any time. The trick is to learn to call up that relaxed, confident state when you need it in the future.

Here's how: Create some kind of signal (rubbing your hands together, tapping your foot, jiggling your club on the ground). Perform this signal, and then vividly imagine one of your great shots discussed above. When the great-shot image elicits its associated mental state of relaxed confidence, that same state will become associated with the signal you have given yourself. If you perform this sequence repeatedly, you will learn to feel relaxed and confident whenever you give yourself that signal. Anchoring should prove very useful during a match when you face a pressure shot that requires an extra measure of relaxation and confidence in achieving success.

Chapter 11

Personality and Attitude

Personality and golf interact in two ways. First, golfers' personalities are put on display on the golf course. Michael Murphy (1972) referred to golf as an "X-ray of the soul," an external reflection of what is going on inside. Golfers simply can't leave their personalities at home. Furthermore, the traits displayed on the course (i.e., timidity, anger, compassion, etc.) are likely to have an impact on the golfers' performance, a relationship which will be the primary focus of this chapter.

But before addressing the personality–performance relationship in more detail, there is another way in which golf and personality interact that should be mentioned. Not only does personality affect golf, but golf can also have an impact on personality. That is, a golfer can use the game as a creative way to experiment with and change his or her personality. Said another way, if modification of one's everyday psychosocial functioning is desired, why not practice new ways of being in the safer confines of the golf course?

For example, perhaps a person has always been a conservative chap, reluctant to take chances, always playing the percentages and taking the safer route. But now he decides he wants a little more excitement out of life, he's tired of settling for a safe second best, he wants to start going for solid accomplishments. Why not try that philosophy out first on the golf course? When the chances of success with a gambling shot seem 50–50, the golfer could go with the gambling 50 instead of his usual safe 50. He might even consider going with the gambling 40 or 30 percent every once in a while; after all, it's only golf.

Now, indeed, the golfer may not always win the gambles and may still come in second, even with the less conservative play. But he will, at least, be behaving like a more adventurous, spirited type of individual and thereby practicing and learning a new type of personality which may be more important in the long run than the golf score.

What other personality traits might be practiced on the golf course? Consider the opposite of the above, the inveterate risk taker practicing a more conservative approach to golf (and life). Golf provides ample opportunities to practice the opposite of anger—calmness and patience—in the face of the many unsettling occurrences the game presents. If a golfer is one who takes a hard-driving, workaholic personality to the golf course, and then proceeds to "play" with the same driven quality, perhaps golf can be a vehicle for developing

MENTAL SPOTLIGHT　The Four Egos

There are four troublesome golfing personalities. Keeping them under control is the key to the proper attitude.

It's easy to detect quirks in a golf swing. Even a beginner can notice a flying right elbow. But it's more difficult to spot personality traits that may impede your progress as a golfer just as much as weaknesses in your swing.

Golfing personalities are numerous. But if I were to select the four most troublesome, I would have to highlight the following:

Cocky Charlie

SYMPTOMS

The cocky golfer perceives winning as beyond his reach, and so he settles for a substitute reward, that of appearing to be a winner. Often, he must engage in intrigue to protect this image.

For example, he often talks about his golfing feats, but he must avoid playing with his audience to maintain his appearance as a winner. If he does get trapped into playing with his audience, he faces insurmountable pressure because of his previous boasting. On the golf course, he takes reckless chances or refuses to accept handicap strokes. In both cases, he has an excuse for losing, and his winning image remains intact. He has physical ailments "on call" as excuses for poor play. He neglects to keep score, avoiding an accurate measure of his ability. Instead, he talks about the highlights of his round.

He uses inappropriate equipment, such as stiff shafts when he needs regular ones, to avoid appearing weak. For the same reason, he often underclubs himself. And, perhaps worst of all, he often tampers with his handicap. An abnormally high one assures him of victory in handicap tournaments; an abnormally low one makes him appear better than he is.

REMEDIES

1. Don't settle for appearing to be a winner, when winning is what counts.
2. Remember that boasting only puts pressure on yourself, and sets you up to fall short of expectations.
3. Be a cool, calculating competitor. Play strategic, percentage golf within your capabilities.
4. Establish an accurate handicap and use it appropriately. Only with an accurate handicap can victory be meaningful.

Superstitious Sydney

SYMPTOMS

In superstitious golfers, some of their personality characteristics may have developed because they have been rewarded somewhere along the line. For example, psychologist Peter Cranford discovered a man who made a point of having a full bladder during his matches. It so happened that the golfer once had won an important match while fighting the pain of a full bladder. Afterward, he believed this uncomfortable physiological state was a prerequisite for victory.

Although this example is humorous, it describes perfectly how some superstitions develop. In other cases, wearing a cowboy hat, carrying a rabbit's foot or eating fried liver and bananas for breakfast may be followed by reward, and thus become a superstition.

The irony is that superstitions usually have little to do with obtaining reward. On the contrary, they may interfere with obtaining rewards. A relatively benign superstition can develop into an incapacitating one, or it can cause the development of a repertoire of distracting superstitious behavior.

Of course, there is a fine line between a distracting superstition and a ritual or action that contributes to victory. A good example is a preshot routine, which many golfers consider essential for consistent play and the maintenance of concentration.

Other golfers insist on using a certain type of golf ball. This, too, has elements of superstition, but also aspects of material worth. It may be that the type of ball a golfer "superstitiously" insists on using also is the best type for his game.

The main point is to guard against letting superstitions become so numerous and time-consuming that they distract you from the important factors in golf, like practice, and make you uncomfortable because of your dependence on irrelevant behavior.

REMEDIES

1. After playing well, analyze the events that occurred before and during the round, and determine which ones contributed *materially* to your success.
2. Continue doing whatever you believe contributed to success, such as practicing, thinking strategically, getting enough rest, etc.
3. While you are "on your game," vary, or even eliminate, those factors which you suspect are superstitious to see if they have any effect on your performance.
4. If the elimination of some suspected superstition seems to hurt your game, analyze it for aspects

continued

MENTAL SPOTLIGHT   *Continued*

which may be useful for good play; i.e., using a certain type of golf ball.

5. If you find that you can't play well without some superstition, then perhaps you should learn to live with it, and with the risk that it may get out of control and become harmful. After all, a little superstition, if it remains benign, is a small price to pay for being able to play good golf.

Masochistic Melvin

SYMPTOMS

This golfer seems to enjoy losing. Some critics say he lacks "the killer instinct," but his problem is worse than that. The masochistic golfer believes he's fated to finish second. Losing brings relief.

The masochistic golfer loses to get something he wants, perhaps sympathy from family and friends. Maybe he has a self-image of a "loser," and wants to verify that image. If he were to win, he would be forced to change his self-image and increase his future expectations to a level he might not think he can maintain. Therefore, he loses simply to avoid the demands of higher expectations.

Last of all, he might lose because he wants to avoid making his opponents unhappy. This is particularly true when the opponent is a club-throwing, complaining hot-head, whose unhappiness causes discomfort for those who must endure it.

The masochistic golfer usually is unaware of his desire to lose. But if someone loses consistently—and seems to enjoy it—he should become aware of the situation. He should then learn to recognize the greater rewards for winning and deny himself the usual rewards for losing.

This assumes, of course, that winning is important. To answer this, I must quote the late Adolph Rupp, the University of Kentucky's great basketball coach, who said, "If it doesn't matter whether you win or lose, then why do they keep score?"

REMEDIES

1. After losing, do not indulge in "consolation prizes" such as sympathy, drowning your sorrow, etc.
2. Don't make or accept excuses for a loss. Excuses will only delay the work necessary for victory.
3. Be a bit of a poor loser. Don't be obnoxious or unfriendly, but don't enjoy losing, either. Treat yourself as a winner who expects to win, but loses occasionally.

4. View golfers who are hot-heads and complainers as golfers who are trying to talk you out of beating them. Beat these manipulative golfers as soundly as you can.
5. "Punish" yourself for losing with immediate extra practice.

Angry Andy

SYMPTOMS

This golfer loses his temper, criticizes the course, blames his clubs for his bogeys, throws clubs, complains about his physical condition, and so on. The development of this type of behavior is rooted in the cognitive dissonance theory.

Social psychologist Leon Festinger, the author of the theory, suggests that when humans are confronted with incompatible thoughts, they behave in such a way as to make their thoughts more consistent.

You might think: "I am a good golfer, yet I hit bad shots." These are incompatible thoughts, and so you must change one of the thoughts to make it consistent with the other.

You have two true alternatives. You can practice enough to start hitting good shots; or you can continue hitting bad shots and admit you are not a good golfer. Neither alternative is acceptable to most golfers, because one requires work and the other requires humility.

So golfers often select a third "alternative." They say to themselves: "I am a good golfer, and other things are to blame for my poor shots." He can blame his deficiencies on something other than himself.

REMEDIES

1. Recognize that complaints only delay the practice you need to improve.
2. Use extra practice as "punishment" for losing your temper.
3. If you do seem doomed to hitting poor shots, you might be wise to accept your limitations instead of creating tension in yourself because of unrealistically high expectations.

Keeping these four golf personalities under control is a key to good golf. In the words of one immortal golfer (whose math wasn't quite as sound as his game), "Golf is 90 per cent mental. Once you get your head straight, you have half the problem licked."

a more relaxed, laid-back type of personality, a way of doing things previously foreign to her.

In all of the above examples, the task involves changing the golfer's goal from shooting the lowest score possible to working on some aspect of personal life. The ironic thing is that as the person focuses on a personality goal, golf scores may improve right along with personality. Two possible explanations for this phenomenon may apply: (1) The personality trait in need of change may have been getting in the way of better performance on the golf course, and/or (2) concentration on something other than score may reduce self-induced pressure and free up the golfer to shoot scores that have thus far been so evasive.

Golf challenges people at every turn to look at themselves and question what they are doing. It also affords the opportunity to change what is being done so as to become a more effective individual. In short, golf offers a prime example of the importance of "how you play the game."

Conservative vs. Risky Golf

If there were a dominant division of personality types on the golf course, it would have to be between those who are conservative and those who are risky. For those who approach the game conservatively, the strategy is one of steadiness, straight down the middle, stay out of trouble, always take the percentage shot. Golfing greats such as Bobby Jones and Jack Nicklaus had tremendously successful careers with this approach.

Other very successful golfers such as Arnold Palmer and Greg Norman have taken a more risky approach to the game. Their games epitomized going for everything, birdie or nothing, always in and out of trouble, recovering from unsuccessful gambles, a "damn the torpedoes" type of existence. They took no prisoners.

The distinction between conservative and risky golf is not a matter of which is best. Both have their virtues. The issue is which approach best fits the golfer's personality. The approach which fits best is the one which will probably feel most comfortable and be most likely to lead to success.

In making this assessment, look at other areas of life. What serves you best in school, business, or your personal life? Are you a person of steady productivity who takes on reasonable tasks and rarely loses and who occasionally hits on something quite outstanding? Or do you always go for the big deal, the major project, winning big or falling flat on your face, leaving the regular work for your less adventurous colleagues?

What about money? Are you a saver or a gambler? If you gamble a bit on investments, are you in the more conservative fixed-income instruments and blue-chip stocks; or do you dabble in the over-the-counter market, buying on margin, in the market one day and out the next, all the while taking substantial risks with your finances?

Regarding family life, are you a steady spouse, parent, or child, with regular activities, always on time, same pleasant vacation every year? Or are you the more flamboyant type, dashing here and there, always coming up with some new activity, taking spontaneous, off-beat vacations?

Indeed, there are virtues to both lifestyles, and perhaps the most adaptive position is to move flexibly between both camps. Still, you probably tend to lean in one direction or

MENTAL SPOTLIGHT   Fit Your Game to Your Personal Values

Students around the country are either planning for or recovering from their mid-year exams. So, it only seems reasonable that we students of golf avail ourselves to some similar self-examination before we embark on the new golf season.

The following is an examination of your golfing values. Many items relate particularly to professional golf, but the areas tapped are ones that any amateur who has paid his dues can identify with. Besides, what amateur has not imagined himself as a pro at one time or another?

So pick your answers and clarify your values. If you want to really have some fun, take it to the 19th hole, and see if you can predict the answers of your golfing colleagues. There are, of course, no right or wrong answers. Only your values are on the line.

1. As a club pro, I would prefer a (a) high-pressured job at a prestigious club, (b) relaxed job at a little-known club.

2. My idea of a good time playing golf would be (a) high-powered tournament, (b) low-key tournament, (c) friendly match with a bunch of old buddies, (d) round by myself.

3. Competitively, I would be more likely to seek out (a) individual competition in a medal play event, (b) individual competition in a match play event, (c) a best-ball team match, (d) a scramble.

4. I would rather (a) qualify for the U.S. Open, but then fail to make the cut, (b) come in tenth in the Buick Open, (c) come in second in the French Open, (d) win my state open championship.

5. I would rather watch a tournament (a) from one location on the golf course, and see all the players pass by, (b) by following one pairing of my choosing for all 18 holes, (c) from my own living room on T.V.

6. If I could have only one, I would prefer (a) one round at a classic course with a prestigious reputation, (b) five rounds at a top calibre course that has no special reputation, (c) ten rounds at my home course.

7. If each of the following cost the same, I would rather (a) take a three-day golfing trip to Scotland, (b) have a one-week vacation at my favorite American golf resort, (c) take a month off and play my home course.

8. I would rather (a) play a mediocre round before a T.V. audience, (b) play extremely well by myself, but have nobody witness any of my great shots.

9. I would rather be a (a) well-known and respected golfer who collected moderate winnings while on tour (i.e., Sam Snead, Ben Hogan), (b) lesser-known and less-respected golfer who is making a small fortune on the present tour.

10. I would rather retire with a record like (a) Andy North, who won two U.S. Opens, but little else, (b) Tom Kite, who won numerous tournaments and was recognized as an excellent golfer, but who won no majors.*

Having answered the above questions, have you noticed any pattern to your responses? Do your choices reflect an intense, individualistic, ambitious golfer, who likes to go for the gold? Or are you more of a laid-back, team-oriented, relaxed kind of golfer who prefers to play the percentages? Maybe you might want to consider making some New Year's resolutions based on what you've learned.

*Note: Since this article was written, Tom Kite has won a major—the 1992 U.S. Open Championship.

the other. No problem; it can be interesting either way. Indeed, it's exciting to go for it, to take a gamble, to do something different, and particularly to hit on a big success. And it's equally satisfying to calmly, methodically, almost surgically, master a situation in precisely the way you planned it.

Golf is a risky game of calculated gambles, unplanned trouble, and miraculous recoveries. But it is also a conservative game benefitting from a repeating swing, keeping the ball in the fairway, and avoiding three-putt greens and double bogeys. Golf can be played with an eye toward knocking the pin down as soon as one gets within 3-wood distance of the green. Or it can be played with percentage shots, assured pars, and birdies that just happen instead of being forced into the hole.

Which approach is chosen is, again, not a matter of which is better. It's more a matter of what your personality is, in general, which is presumably the style you are comfortable with and believe in—be it either conservative or risky. Why not let that effective personality that is working for you elsewhere be an additional asset for you on the golf course?

Attitude Change and Game Improvement

Just as there are two general personality types (conservative vs. risky), two general attitudes toward the game might also be identified. Most simply stated, these attitudes are *positive* or *negative*. But contrary to the mutually beneficial aspects of the two personality types, there is only one good attitude: positive.

The positive attitude is more aggressive. Each hole is an opportunity. Each shot might go in the hole. If the golfer messes up, she is expecting a great comeback. If the comeback fails to materialize, she takes it in stride. The golfer doesn't become disgruntled, blaming herself, the course, or environmental conditions. She has a positive attitude, is out there to win; but if winning isn't to be, she can still have fun.

The negative attitude is more defensive. Each hole is a threat. The negative golfer is just hoping to get the ball somewhere near the green. There is no thought of actually reaching the putting surface. When the player messes up, it is total calamity. If he doesn't blame himself for his stupidity, any outside agent within 3-wood distance may incur his wrath. The golfer with a negative attitude is out there to avoid losing, out there to survive.

One way a negative attitude can affect the game is in planning shots as if they are going to be hit less than well. For example, a golfer may be expecting to hook the ball, even though he is trying to hit it straight. As he addresses the ball, he unconsciously waggles the stance around until he is aiming right of the target to allow for a hook. Now, of course, he *has* to hook it to achieve the desired result. But he is still trying to hit it straight. All of these conflicting thoughts create considerable confusion for the brain, which passes on some equally jumbled messages to the body that is supposed to execute the shot. The legs, hips, arms, and hands don't know whether to hit it straight or hook it, and in all likelihood will end up hitting the ball fat, i.e., hitting behind the ball resulting in a fat chunk of earth traveling farther than the ball.

Speaking of hitting it fat, another example of this type of negative thinking would be overclubbing (i.e., hitting a club that is likely to hit the ball farther than required) because the golfer is not expecting to hit a crisp, clean shot. In other words, if she hits enough club, maybe she can get away with the slightly fat shot she'll probably hit. Once again, this golfer has maneuvered herself into a confusing position where she *has* to hit it fat or risk flying the ball 20 yards over the green. Such confusion between brain and body cannot lend itself to an aggressive, confident swing.

Jack Nicklaus exemplified the contrast between positive and negative thinking in an interview during the 1989 U.S. Open. He had just put the finishing touches on a first round 67 and was reflecting on his strategy. That strategy was, "Why not go out and make the ball go where you want it to go?" He continued, "A high percentage of rounds, you stand up to the ball when you're not hitting as well as you would like and say to yourself, 'Where is the best place for me to miss?' Today I had a more positive attitude. It was fun." The following are some suggestions for generating a positive attitude:

1. Best shot. Play each shot like you are going to hit your best shot. Select the club that, if hit well, will be the appropriate club for the given shot. Then proceed to put your best move on the ball and be surprised if it doesn't come out perfect. If the distance is such that you are having difficulty deciding between two clubs (e.g., between a 7 or an 8 iron), consider taking the shorter club, concentrating all the more, and putting an even better move on the ball than you would if you were playing it safe. Play the percentages, but don't get all twisted up allowing for too much error.

2. Friendly hole. Think of each hole as a friend that is coaxing you to knock each shot down the middle of the fairway and ultimately into the hole. There is more room in the fairway than in the combined area of the bordering strips of rough. The fairway is like a magnet just waiting for the ball to be drawn to it. So hang a shot out over that magnetic, welcoming path to success.

Although this may sound a little overdone, it may be just the exaggeration that is necessary to overcome negative thoughts like, "Oh no, not this monster again!" Furthermore, don't abandon this mental attitude if your best friends (or fairways) let you down occasionally. Even best friends are not perfect. It may take time to really understand and depend on each other.

3. Comeback opportunity. If you do mess up during a round, view this as simply an opportunity to make a comeback. Consider that many of the great moments in sports are comebacks. Historically, if all the football teams who were 20 or 30 points down in the second half had given up, many would have been deprived of the thrill of making tremendous comebacks.

Do you want to miss your opportunity for a great comeback? Don't give up the next time the round demands a little character on your part. Just say to yourself, "This may be my time, my opportunity for the comeback of a lifetime. Wouldn't it be a shame if I missed it by giving up at this point?"

4. Realistic optimism. Engage in realistic optimism rather than in phony positive thinking. If you approach the game of golf saying to yourself, "I am the greatest golfer that ever lived and there is no way anything can go wrong today," *it won't work*. That is phony positive thinking. The mind cannot totally be fooled. It will recognize a blatant lie.

However, you can benefit from realistic optimism such as, "I've been practicing a lot and I am hitting the ball well. There is no reason that some well-planned shots can't be put together for a good round today. I'll undoubtedly run into my share of trouble, but recovery shots and a few hard-earned pars are all part of a good round. I'm ready to go out and show what I can do."

5. Win the game. Remember that golf is a game, and that games are meant to be won. Thirty minutes after the contest, nobody remembers who came in second, tenth, or last. So go for the win. Take some risks, make things happen.

As General Douglas MacArthur reportedly said, "There is no security in this world, only opportunity." The same can be said for golf. If players walk too timidly and try to protect themselves from impending doom, the course will eventually up and grab them. But if they assert themselves, more opportunity may be found than was ever expected.

Delaying Gratification

Golf, like life, often involves delaying gratification, which is a fancy term for patience. Whatever it's called, waiting for something can be difficult. Children have a hard time waiting for Christmas, or birthdays, or simply the visit of a cherished friend or relative. Teenagers covet new cars and status in the community before they have put in the time and effort necessary to earn those things. Even adults want to have things before they can afford them, unable to postpone the pleasure of ownership until they have earned the money to pay for the desired items. Indeed, the credit card industry is largely supported by people's inability to delay gratification. Perhaps the premier example of unwillingness to delay gratification is the motto that was attributed to one of the more affluent areas of the country: "I want it *all*, and I want it *now*!"

As with so many personality traits, the inability to delay gratification is just one more trait that is taken to the golf course. In various ways and at various phases of the game golfers say, "I want it all, and I want it now."

For example, practice is an activity which involves delaying gratification. The rationale for saying this is that the primary gratification in golf is a low score, which can only be obtained by actually playing a round of golf. To practice means to forego playing a round of golf, thereby incurring a delay in receiving the potential gratification of a low score. Of course, the hope is that by practicing and delaying gratification, the reward will be even greater when a lower score is produced during future play. But golfers have a hard time believing this.

Another aspect of golf that involves delaying gratification is in exercising patience over an entire 18-hole round. A golfer starts off with a couple of pars and immediately gets excited as if having already shot a 72. This is in contrast to patiently investing time and effort into an entire 18-hole round and saving the celebrating, both internally and externally, until all the work is done.

Yet another example of inability to delay gratification is looking up too soon after a shot. Golfers often can't wait even a fraction of a second to see the hoped for result and feeling of reward. Of course, when they don't wait that fraction of a second, the reward, if any, is greatly diminished in the form of the poor shot that is actually seen.

The moral of all this is that if you can't delay gratification, you often won't get any gratification at all. The golfer who is unwilling to practice, who can't patiently complete a round, or who insists on looking up from the ball prematurely usually ends up with less than gratifying results. The individual who "wants it all and wants it now," often ends up with nothing, both now and in the future.

Ironically, the solution to this difficulty does not actually require delaying gratification. It requires redefining gratification. Instead of viewing gratification as exclusively the final, perfect product toward which one is striving, it can be noted that there are many smaller gratifications along the way to ultimate success.

For example, there is gratification in practicing well. Practice scores can be kept to provide feedback as to how a certain skill is developing. Regarding patience over an 18-hole round, calculation of three-hole scores, as described in Chapter Ten, might be useful in building a series of successes if it is hard to wait for the final accounting.

For the most difficult challenge of them all—keeping the head down—immediate gratification might be obtained by visualizing a beautiful shot during the fraction of a second that is spent staying down over the ball. Furthermore, the ultimate gratification is likely to soon follow in the form of seeing an approximation of that beautiful visualization in reality when one does finally look to see the result.

Control of Temper

Golfers all have a tendency to get angry on the golf course. They throw clubs or bang them on the ground after bad shots, berate themselves verbally for their inconsistent play, gnash their teeth or grimace, or just give up and quit. Sometimes quitting involves physically leaving the course; other times it's more of a psychological departure, merely playing with an "I don't care" attitude.

Of course, this behavior could be evidence of a personality flaw, or it could merely stem from a lack of experience with the game. It may be that these golfers just haven't played enough to know how hard the game is, that inconsistency and bad shots are inevitable, or that quitting is nonproductive and only robs one of the opportunity for thrilling comebacks.

To compound the problem, golfers sometimes seem to operate as if they were invisible on the golf course, as if they can do anything they want and nobody will see them. Perhaps it would help them to control their tempers if they were to consider what they are communicating to others every time they lose it.

For example, when a golfer displays her temper on the golf course, she is in effect trying to say "I'm a good player, even though my game is not reflecting it at the moment." Rather than focusing on the task and letting her game show how good she is, she thinks she can talk others into believing it by her display of anger. In contrast, consider the touring pro who misses a shot on national TV. Of course, she's not happy, but what she does is take on a look of determination that quietly says, "Wait till the next hole and you'll see how good I am. I don't have to kick and scream. My clubs will do the talking."

A second thing a golfer does when he gets angry is to broadcast to his opponents (and everybody else) that he has been beaten. It's like a fighter who starts crying; the other fighter knows he's got him beat. Furthermore, all the opponent has to do is keep the crybaby mad, and he'll beat himself.

A third consideration is that when a golfer recklessly displays her emotions, she risks not only losing the game but also losing her image in the community. Unfortunately, all a person has to do is make a fool of herself one time, and it's amazing how hard it is for observers to forget. They may understand, and may even have done it themselves, but it still affects their impression of the person from then on. This seems particularly important for young golfers who are just beginning to establish themselves in the educational, employment, and social communities. Golf may be important, but other things will become increasingly important as the years go by.

Two other considerations may help golfers moderate their emotional reactions to the game: Unless a golfer is devoting extensive practice time to the game, he shouldn't expect to beat those who are. Some golfers who are playing only occasionally go out on a given day and expect to beat those who are practicing and playing daily. The occasional golfer may, indeed, be a good golfer, quite capable of beating the others. But, until he has had time to practice and play as much as his opponents, he should be patient and content with just giving them a run for their money.

The other suggestion is for golfers to avoid competition that is doomed to produce frustration. That is, a golfer should win the local tournaments before tackling the state amateur championship where she is doomed to failure considering her present stage of development. It's a lot more fun to win something small than to get clobbered in something big. It's a lot easier on the emotions, too!

The Dreaded Club Championship

Whether a golfer plays regularly at one of the many fine public courses in the country or is a member of an elite country club, there is an annual ritual that provides an interesting study in the psychology of golf. It is known as the club championship: the ultimate theater for personality and golf.

During this event one can witness grown men trembling, laughing nervously, sweating profusely, and, in general, having a hard time enjoying themselves in their usual weekend manner. The typically stoic, stable, self-assured businessman, who is always well in control of himself and his game, suddenly comes apart under the pressure of the club championship.

To carry the description of events a bit further, there seem to be at least four groups of golfers who emerge during the club championship: First, there are those who practice and play all year long. They sign up for the tournament as soon as it is announced and they continue to prepare diligently for the competition. This is the most admirable group, but the least interesting, because they are doing just what one would expect. They are anxious about the competition, but they confront it bravely and accept the eventual outcome.

The second group, on the other hand, is the most interesting. They practice and play all year long, but they don't sign up for the club championship. Some of these are very good golfers, and it bewilders many that they are not playing in the tournament. This group's behavior might be explained by: (1) a lack of motivation due to feeling that they are too good for the competition; (2) fear that they can't live up to their stellar reputations as skilled golfers; or (3) inability to handle the pressure because of their exclusive involvement in social golf rather than formal competition.

The third group provides an element of surprise. These are the players who don't practice or play much all year but who suddenly show up for the club championship. They race out, hit a bag of balls, and maybe play nine holes the evening before the tournament, subsequently declaring themselves "ready to go." Sometimes they seem to come out of the woodwork (or, in the case of golf, out of the woods). There is the desire to say, "What are you doing here? I haven't seen you all year!" These players are hardly worth analyzing. They are out for a party. There is no pressure on them. Neither they nor anyone else expects them to be any threat to the crown.

The fourth group is more subtle and sometimes goes unnoticed. These are the players who come in at the last minute to sign up. They either just make it or don't make it at all.

They are the procrastinators, the ones who take an impulsive plunge at the last minute. Like the second group, these golfers are probably afraid; but instead of staying away altogether, they leave it up to fate. They say to themselves, "Well, if I can still get in, I'll reluctantly play; but if I'm too late to sign up, that's quite all right, too."

Why does the club championship elicit such fear and anxiety among otherwise emotionally stable humans? Frankly, I think the anxiety is understandable and justifiable. First, there is no audience that induces more pressure than the hometown crowd. They have known the competitors for a lifetime, and they are not easily impressed. Although the tournament players may be highly respected in other circles, their everyday peers know all the mistakes they have made for a lifetime. With the presence of the hometown crowd, the competitors are up against their most formidable critics, a situation which provides a justifiable basis for anxiety.

Second, because the club championship is an annual event, the competitors know they have only this single opportunity per year to display their individual talents. Sure, they will play in other events, but most of these events will be team competitions where individual scores are hidden in a team total. But in the club championship, one time per year, golfers have to put their individual scores on the board. That's intimidating. Not even the pros face that kind of one-shot pressure. The pros know that if they blow it this week, they can come back next week and show that they can play better, which is not the case in the club championship. Club golfers have to wait a whole year to have another chance to demonstrate their individual, golfing self-worth. That is a lot of pressure.

So go the psychological gymnastics of the club championship. And thus it will continue until players accept the fact that golf is a difficult game and quit apologizing for scores in the 80s and 90s. Indeed, acceptance of the difficulty of the game would go a long way toward eliminating unrealistic expectations, which lead to so much anxiety in golf.

The club pro might help alleviate some of the anxiety by explaining beforehand that players might expect to shoot somewhat higher scores because of the unusual pressure of the competition. To back this up, the pro might provide some statistics from previous club championships so that players get a realistic perspective on the range of scores that have been shot in the past under these conditions.

This is not to suggest that the pro discourage the players in their quest for excellence. Rather, it is to suggest that the pro encourage the players to be realistic, keep the competition in perspective, and continue trying even when their games take unusual turns. The pro should go out of his way to applaud the participants for their willingness to put themselves on the line in this intense competition, whatever the outcome might be.

The ultimate remedy for reducing tournament anxiety is for golfers to seek out regular, individual competition throughout the year. By doing so, they have more chances to post their scores, see how they compare with other players, get used to the pressure, and not be so overwhelmed by the awesome mystique of the *club championship*.

References

Bandura, A. (1969). *Principles of Behavior Modification.* New York: Holt, Rinehart & Winston.

Clark, L. V. (1960). "Effect of mental practice on the development of a certain motor skill." *Research Quarterly, 31,* 560–569.

Cranford, P. G. (1961) *The Winning Touch in Golf.* Englewood Cliffs, NJ: Prentice-Hall.

Dorsel, T. N. (1978) "A mastery learning approach to practicing athletic skills." *Perceptual and Motor Skills, 46,* 1243–1246.

Dorsel, T. N., and Salinsky, D. M. (1990) "Enhancing willingness to practice golf through use of a mastery approach." *Perceptual and Motor Skills, 70,* 415–418.

Frank, J. A. (1991) "The new basics." *GOLF Magazine, 33,* 29–42.

Jobe, F. W., and Schwab, D. R. (1986). *30 Exercises for Better Golf.* Inglewood, CA: Champion Press.

Jones, E. (1952) *Swing the Clubhead.* New York: Dodd, Mead and Company, Inc.

King, M., Novik, L., and Citrenbaum, C. (1983) *Irresistible Communication: Creative Skills for the Health Professional.* Philadelphia: W. B. Saunders Company.

Miller, G. A. (1956) "The magical number seven, plus or minus two: Some limits on our capacity for processing information." *Psychological Review, 63,* 81–97.

Murphy, M. (1972) *Golf in the Kingdom.* New York: Arkana.

Orlick, T., and Partington, J. (1988) "Mental links to excellence." *The Sport Psychologist, 2,* 105–130.

Pelz, D., with Frank, J. A. (1990) "The 3 X 4 system." *GOLF Magazine, 32,* 68–75.

Penick, H., with B. Shrake (1992) *Harvey Penick's Little Red Book.* New York: Simon and Schuster.

United States Golf Association and Royal and Ancient Golf Club of St. Andrews (1995) *Rules of Golf.* Far Hills, NJ: Golf House.

United States Golf Association (1993) "Handicaps of U.S. golfers." *GOLFWEEK, 19,* #22, 1.

Vardon, H. (1905) *The Complete Golfer.* New York: McClure, Phillips.

Vealey, R. S., and Walter, S. M. (1993) "Imagery training for performance enhancement and personal development." In J. M. Williams (Ed.), *Applied Sport Psychology: Personal Growth to Peak Performance* (204–205). Mountain View, Calif.: Mayfield Publishing Company.

Watson, T., with Hannigan, F. (1988) *The New Rules of Golf.* New York: Random House.

Wiren, G., Coop, R., with Sheehan, L. (1978) *The New Golf Mind.* Norwalk, CT: Golf Digest, Inc.

Index

10103

1108